MEATY
MONOLOGUES

THE MONOLOGUES &
ONE-PERSON PLAYS OF
JANE SHEPARD

Cover Photo: Tom Johnson in
"Glass Jaw" (photo Travis McHale)

This book is independently published, and your support goes
directly to the author, empowering creative independence and feistiness

.

ISBN: 978-0-557-01276

For permission visit www.kickass-plays.com, or write to the playwright c/o 404 Hapgood, Boulder, CO 80302.

TABLE OF CONTENTS

All monologues & short plays in this book are by Jane Shepard, and are drawn from her plays and screenplays. Some are available for production, and your inquiries are welcome. To produce any of the included plays, you need written permission from the playwright.

To request a script, contact the playwright, or find out more about Jane Shepard's work, visit

www.JaneShepardArt.com

OF MONOLOGUES: WHY DO THEY SUCK?

by Jane Shepard

What is it with monologues? I don't know how many you've had the chance to see in your life, but have you noticed that some speeches have a way of grabbing you by the collar and giving you a good delightful shake, while others just sit there and suck? And by sucking I don't mean the heinously bad; those are at least morbidly fascinating. I mean the ones where you're kinda bored, and it seems sorta long, and the actor is working awful hard, and if it lasts much longer, well, at least you have that loose piece of sneaker to play with. Why do some thrill & some not? And wouldn't it be nice to know *before* you're up on stage, delighting people or watching them flap a loose chunk of shoe? Or are just stuck reading some.

Sucky monologues are a subject I've spent many long luxurious hours debating with my friends Shawn Hirabayashi and Julie Hamberg, a fellow playwright and director respectively. Our quest to define a good monologue has stretched into years. As members of Circle Repertory Company in its final years, we were the last generation to benefit from one of New York's original developmental companies. We participated in the playwrights' group, and brought new works to the Lab, which boasted 300 writers, directors and actors all in service of first stagings. We attended Circle in the Square, the Off-Broadway house where the best scripts went to production; and we relished the playwright's retreats that Lanford Wilson was kind enough to host at his house. We emerged with more than ample exposure to monologues, and our conclusions varied not a whit from yours: some sucked and some were good meat. But the elements that comprised a successful monologue remained largely undefined. And so it was left to Shawn, Julie & I to sort out amongst ourselves.

First we considered the actor. Was it the performer that made the monologue? We were blessed with fantastic actors at the Circle Rep lab, and they often compensated for a bevy of script iniquities. But saddle them with a wordy, boring, shapeless speech, and you've got a Rolls Royce delivering pizza. So if it wasn't the actor, did success depend on the amount of truth and passion in the writing? Maybe, but you can find plenty of plays written with great earnestness and packed with significant subjects. Regardless of heartfelt intent – or maybe because of it – it's a short slip & fall into the puddle of political proselytizing or regretful remembrance. In fact, the word 'remembrance' gave us shivers anywhere a monologue was concerned. That, we discovered, was the one thing we could all agree on! None of us ever wanted to hear another monologue that began, *"When I was a growing up...", "Back in my hometown ..."* or even, *"I remember when it happened..."*

Why the dread of past tense? Had we become shallow cads who despised reflection? What's wrong with having a character tell something that happened to them? Lots of great plays are based on recalling a significant event, and plenty of monologues are people reviewing their history. What else is there to do in a speech?

If you've acted in a play, or directed one, or even *seen* one, you know the goal is a sort of dramatic unfolding. It requires tension: conflict between the characters or with opposing circumstance. (In the best cases, both!) Sometimes the action of the play is physical, like having a sword fight onstage or, in the case of Peter Shaffer's **Equus**, running around blinding horses. In other plays the action is emotional: falling in love, figuring things out, or in Marsha's Norman's **'night, mother**, debating suicide. That's Emotional Action. In any case, the conflict comes to a climax, and then to a resolution, where we finally understand how the characters have been changed by the experience.

When a character stands onstage telling a past-tense story, it has remarkably similar ingredients to a dramatic unfolding. There's probably a conflict in that story, and it has a climax and resolution. The teller often experiences emotional upheaval in telling it. These similarities make it seem like we've been given a dramatic experience. The only catch is, nothing has happened on stage! Even if the story-teller has been darting around doing interesting things, the actual drama did not happen in front of you, in the present. The tension is only being recalled. Maybe the storyteller was moved, but are they *changed* by telling it? In the laziest monologues, we don't even know *why* the character is telling the story, or *who* they're supposed to be talking to, much less how the telling will alter them.

There's a difference between 'recalled action' as opposed to 'action in the play'. It's very easy to confuse them, and it's probably one of the most common mistakes monologue writers make. Without a pressing need for the character to relate the story, there's nothing at stake. And if there's nothing preventing them from telling it, there's also no conflict. What is there for us to root for? We're watching the story of someone telling a story. And although it may be an interesting story, there's no action in the present, and pretty soon we're playing with that loose flap of sneaker.

Yo ho, there lies the challenge of a good monologue! Avoiding *Sneaker-Flap Syndrome*. Whether it's a speech in the middle of a play, a one-person show, or a monologue for class, there should be an action for the character in the present.

One that leaves them in a different place emotionally by the end. And that is quite a challenge. Since a monologue is only one person, there probably isn't going to be a swordfight. So mostly the action is going to be emotional. If it involves the character telling a story, there must be a *need* to tell it and, for maximum tension, a conflict in talking about it. Trying to overcome the conflict provides emotional progression, and that will leave them changed by the end.

Of the monologues included here, **A Rage of Chaos** is an example of a character having conflict in telling the story *("Thermometer of Thrills", "Elysian Fields",* also printed in its entirety in the short plays section.*)* In **Rage** a man returns to the weekend retreat he frequented with his circle of friends, all but him now deceased. Although the immediate objective is trying to get served breakfast, his real need is to come to terms with the present, while valiantly trying to avoid the one thing that can help him do that: acknowledging the past. It allows the character to talk about the past, but the struggle is in the present.

Another sort of Emotional Action in a monologue is the *'What will I do next?'* kind. The monologue is a vehicle that will purportedly help them determine their next action. In **Subway**, two women hook up for an anonymous tryst on a late-night subway platform. Both are desperate for human connection, yet both are fearfully resistant: Alice being married & cheating on her husband, and Darcy emotionally frozen by the traumatic death of her partner. In some cases, like Alice's *"Guava"* speech, the fun is in watching the character protest while simultaneously talking herself into it. Darcy *("The Nameless Lips"* and *"Dropped & Bopped")* defends her resistance to intimacy, yet we know the very act of explaining herself will bring them closer. In both cases their internal conflict makes it fun to see where the monologue will leave them by its end.

What about speeches where almost the entire thing is back-story? There are such cases in this book, including Win's falling in love account, *"But When We Saw Each Other",* and Roy's *"Do You Know What Happened to Me Today?!"* speech from **Long Distance** (also printed in the short plays section.) These are almost entirely telling back-story. They demonstrate a third kind of Emotional Action, which is Exploratory. Something has happened that makes a character need to take stock: explore where they stand. Although they are processing the past, it is helping them to understand something about now, providing a new perspective or realization. An audience will travel the past with a character if they feel it has bearing on now. Very often the exploration leads to insight or change the character needs.

So! A good monologue needs 1) Action, even if it's Emotional Action, and 2) a Conflict in the present, and 3) Change or emotional progression that leaves them in a new place by the end. That doesn't seem like so much to ask. Why it took me years to figure out is another matter (or monologue.) It shouldn't be such a difficult thing for us to write, or for you to find. Mostly a matter of knowing what ingredients to look for. And for my conclusions thus far, I want to thank my friends Julie and Shawn for serving up the question in the first place, along with abiding conversation and a whole lotta sodies.

I hope letting you in on the conversation will give you a head start in finding a monologue that has all the right ingredients for you. Because the final necessary element, in addition to action in the present and room for progression, is finding something that voices some of your own truth. *That's* when the experience of theater can become transformative. For audience, and actor. And hey, finding that truth goes for more than just monologues! (Good old art, there's always a life metaphor right around the corner.)

Whether it's a monologue or your larger purpose in life, watch you don't find yourself just flappin' a loose shoe. Go out and find the thing that grabs you by the collar & gives you a good delightful shake. If the experience leaves you transformed, that is meaty indeed!

- Jane Shepard

*For actors seeking particular kinds of roles,
check out the Casting Tables in the back.*

"Such Stuff As Dreams Are Made On"

From *Midsummer Madness*

Scene: A director addresses the cast before the first read-through.

ROBIN:

(Holding script of "A Midsummer Night's Dream")

This script has been around longer than you've been alive. Longer than kingdoms and wars and whole nations. It has *not* survived because it is an entertainment, video games are an entertainment. And when was the last time you played 'Donkey Kong?'

(Holds up script.)

This is timeless because it is the truth. Some poor schmuck picked up a Bic, opened a vein & out poured the truth of all our dreams! And here it is. Read. For this is his blood. And if you think it signifies any less than the wine at Gethsemane, consider this. No psalm ever got a standing ovation. No war hero's name is known around the world & written in every language.

And make no mistake, this *will* be a war. And that *is* a sacred text. If you don't have the stomach for it, quit now. Stand up, get your bag and walk out, no harm done. Art demands your soul. You will not come late to rehearsals. Don't not bother to show up unprepared. Do not *bore* me with the details of your little lives, I don't care. I don't care that your job kept you late serving the masses -- *This* serves the masses!

(Pointing to cast members)

You and you and you and you *will* become such stuff as dreams are made on! Will you be the warriors of these words? Will you fight for the right to speak your hearts through this timeless text? For if you will, oh my children, I guarantee! Those poor slobs at home tonight & in their beds will curse the day they were not cast, to do this show, to speak their hearts, to fight with us, for your stupendous play!

"Guava"

From *Subway*

Scene: Alice is having second thoughts after making out on a late night subway platform with a stranger she picked up at the gym..

ALICE:

This whole thing is my fault. I'm the one that came onto you, you didn't do it. I mean that's why I liked you. You were lifting weights, and you were just so.. indifferent. Your shirt was so baggy, and your shorts were so old, nobody could even see your body under there. But you knew it was there, and just the little bits one could see, it's very sexy, oh my God, you're so sexy – No! I mean it's worse than sexy, it's criminal! You should just wear tight spandex with loud colors like other women. Tight things that leave nothing to the imagination. I just hate those bright colors. It's just total over-sell. It's lurid. No, it's not even lurid, it's oversell. It's like some-body trying to force fruit on you. "Here, have a guava, you don't want a guava? But they're so ripe, so perfect, here, I insist, have this, take it with you, come on, eat it!" *Please!* I just don't want it! Take your, ick, creepy fruit and ick!

But you, what you wear is much worse! It's intriguing. It creates interest. If you didn't want interest, you shouldn't have dressed like that, in that "I don't care" sort of way. I think you know it makes people crazy. I think you know perfectly well you have a fantastic body, and you just flaunt it by hiding it! Where are we? I have to go. What train are we at? No, nevermind, I'll take a taxi. Are you okay? Do you need money?

"The Hole"

From *Glass Jaw*

Scene: Jeff, a young case worker, comes to pay a home visit on a disturbed client and is taken hostage by the client & his sister. They challenge Jeff's values & sanity until he finally confronts the truth of his life.

JEFF:

Okay, you win, you kissed me, it scared the shit out of me. But you wanna know what was really terrifying? The complete lack of meaning behind it. You dominated me, I get it. Dominate all of happy land. Does that mean anything? Is it something significant I can take with me out into the world? 'Cause that's where I live. And I don't get to pick it or create it, and I sure don't control it. But I walk it.

I get up. I go to work, I pay the bills. I buck up. Buck up, Jeff, be a man! Don't sit on your ass dreaming all day, get out & make a goddamn difference in someone's life! Well ya know what? I have no clue how to do that. I don't even know how to make a difference in my own life. And I don't even know *why* I don't know. I took the steps, I got the degree. You follow the signs that are supposed to lead to a significant life. Do not come without that.

I am pretty sure there's not supposed to be a hole where the meaning should be. I may be 'minty', but at least I have the guts to say that. Ya do what you love & you're not contributing, but you try and contribute & and they wanna cut your throat. And somewhere in contending with all that, something begins to fall away & get lost, that turns out to have been you. 'Till some days the only thing that even lets you know you're alive is the rain on your head. But at least *I've* felt the rain.

"But When We Saw Each Other"

From *Strange Grace*

Scene: Win's lover's Bob suffers from physical disabilities & a nervous condition. Here Win recalls the event that caused it.

WIN:

I wish I had a dime for every poor suicidal nutcake who came in here. Most of the them have the consideration not to do it here. Except for Jim. Poor ol' Jimmie. Married himself a hooker and thought he had it made. Quickie wedding at an all-night chapel. Had just enough gas to make it to his brother's place in the desert. I thought I had it good with Jim. He wasn't mean, and he laughed at my jokes.

But when Bob opened that door and we saw each other, I swear, I was so clueless I didn't even know what it was. I thought maybe I was getting the flu. Somebody just looks at you, and it's like they're seeing right through your eyes and down into your soul. Some people go their whole lives and never feel that. And I find it in the middle of the night, in the middle of the desert, right after I just finished marryin' his brother.

And we didn't touch, we didn't shake hands, Jesus, after a couple of minutes we tried to not even look at each other in the room. But we were all over each other in the nooks and crannies of just breathing! And after a couple hours Jim knew it too, and it made him wanna, you know, take me outside and have what was his. And I just, couldn't go back like it was before and be an animal. So, turned out Jim could be mean.

I don't know where the gun came from. By then my eye was swelled shut & they were shouting. And then next thing I know it was going off and blowing Bob apart. If I'd just gone, if we could've made it to the car, everything would've been different. But I swear, I wouldn't have left that place except in a body bag. All I wanted was to stand in the center of the universe for the rest of my entire life with this guy who made me feel like me. If Jim had pulled the trigger on me, I'd have had no complaints. Take me to Graceland, Moses, or throw me in the flames, 'cause I had one good long stare into the eyes of heaven, and nobody and nothing can take that away.

"I Feel My Fingers Creeping About My Face"

From *This Year of Our Lord*

Scene: Lady Malcolm takes confidence in the new neighbor.

LADY MALCOLM:

I am not a bad woman. No, my dear, not a wicked person. Never cruel or suspicious. Au contraire, I have always striven to conduct my life in a delicate vein.

But, let us be frank... yes... no woman is all lady, no female all woman. I am that lady, that woman, like Eve, like Delilah, like..that woman who did the doody with the president but she always had extremely nice hair -- I am no God! Beautiful, yes, kind, caring, adored, effervescent, puckish and a delight, yes, but!... There have been nights.

Oh my God, the long nights. When John lies beside me on his pillow, his face open and smoothed of the day's worries. It seems he would never notice me, silent in the night, lying beside him in my flowing nightdress.

I try to control myself. I try! I study the canopy above, I, I stare at John's digital computer wristwatch! And then, for no reason whatsoever, except that it seems at this late lonely hour I might go unnoticed if I slip just a little, I put my thumbs to my ears and softly, oh so softly as I can, I say...

> *(Puts fingers to ears and makes soft raspberries at John.)*

Oh God, I know it's wrong! But he sleeps so soundly, not a care in his doldrum bald head, and I want to grab it and say...

> *(Mimes grabbing his head.)*

"Baldy, baldy, baldy!" – And then, before I can stop myself, my eyes grow round, round like flying saucers and I shout...

> *(Makes face and noise)*

Then John is awake and startled, just as he always is, in his Pierre Cardin pajamas, and his face strains to summon some iota of expression but he never looks anything but *bland*, and I feel my fingers creeping about my face and suddenly I say, "Looky!"

> *(Makes another face and noise)*

- continues -

LADY MALCOLM: *(cont'd)*

And when he looks I say, "Looky looky!"

(Another face and noise)

And then again, "Looky, looky, looky!"

(Another face and noise)

And then I know John has seen me! And I feel so dreadful that I pull my gown up over my face and, summoning what little composure I have, I say in as casual a voice as I can muster, "...Nevermind."

"Do You Know What Happened to Me Today?!"

From *Long Distance*

Scene: Returning home, Roy addresses the audience as an intimate.

ROY:

Do you know what happened today? Oh! I couldn't wait to tell you! You will die! Do you know who I saw? Fatima Farterweigh! From the third grade? Can you imagine?! Fat Fatima! – Oh, not fat, I shouldn't say fat, um... pudgy – no, Rubenesque. *Rubenesque* Fatima Farterweigh, imbedded into our class picture with brillo hair and her tongue up her nose, one eye going this way and one eye going that. And today I am walking across the plaza, and this, this petrified photographic image is transformed before memory's eye into a living, breathing, grown-up Fatima Farterweigh!

And do you know what she did? She pointed at me and shouted, "Roy!" And I tried to pretend that I hadn't seen her, but she chased me across the plaza screaming, "Roy Gannoy!" Until I shouted back, "I don't know you, and for God's sake, Fatima, stop screaming!" Oh! Can you believe it? I am so lame! But I was absolutely cornered! And she says, "I remember you, you're Roy Gannoy, that boy who talked to himself all alone on the play-ground!" Well. I just turned to her and said, "And you're Fat Fatima who's going to fart-her-way to fourth grade!" And she stopped and said, "But that was mean."

And I said, "No, it was witty." This is a common misconception. If you're a man you can be witty, but if you have ironic insight as an eight-year-old, you're mean. And then she, she who has to shop for clothes at the blimp factory, sort of grins and says, "I was mean too. I just didn't know how to tell anybody I liked them. Did you?" I said, "I never liked anybody."

And she said, "Oh, that's sad." Can you imagine? I said, "No. It's not. It's witty." And she said, "No, Roy, that's sadder than me." "But, you're Fat Fatima Fart-her-way to the fourth grade, wall-eyed & licked your nose in the picture and everybody hated you, even me." "I know," she said, "But I liked you."

"Sex in Droves"

From *Commencing*

Scene: Kelli's much-anticipated blind date has turned out to be a lesbian named Arlin. Appalled, disappointed and uncomfortable, Kelli's been drinking too much.

KELLI:

(Continuing to talk to Arlin, even though Arlin's in the bathroom. In fact, the closed door emboldens her...)

Have you really not had sex in longer than me? Well, that's okay, it doesn't really matter whether you've had someone more recently than me or not. Wouldn't be hard. You could've made love with somebody two *seasons* ago and it would still have me beat. It's just... it would be comforting to know. Because you start to feel like you're the only celibate person on earth. Well, not exactly celibate, but...singular.

(No longer necessarily to Arlin)

And meantime everybody else is having sex in *droves!* Even women who say they aren't, the very next weekend they meet a cute guy and sleep with him, and then they turn out to have the most grotesquely joyous fling! And next thing you know they're getting married, in a pastel colors theme, and everybody's *really* excited, because she waited *so* long for the *right* guy and it's *so* great! Only the happy couple don't know whether to invite you, because they can't remember if they were originally your friends or Ric's. And if they invite Ric, can they invite you too, do you & Rick get along now, or is it just possible that you still want to *cut his dick off with a dull scissors!* Suffice it to say, I am not attracting quite the same dating scene I did before.

"You Got To Have Somethin'"

From *Fiona's Mane*

Scene: A man in recovery is on his way to blow it by buying drugs, when a delay in subways causes him to strike up a conversation with a woman who is even lonelier than he is.

SHAQUAY:

Just seem to me a lonely way to go. No cats, no plants, no men... don't you got nothin' alive in your house? Yeah I know, I know, you think they got germs, but that ain't germs, it's just life. Well, some of it is, some of it ain't clean, but, I'm sorry, you just can't live like that. You got to have a warm body. How else you know you alive yourself? I mean, the soul is a livin' thing, it got to have food, you know what I mean? You go fuckin' with your life, you gonna be all alone. Just a empty room, you just a empty room, nobody wanna be there with you, nobody comin' there, nobody need that. You be so alone. And you may *think* it don't make you no mind, but after a time you ain't gonna wanna be there yourself. And then it's only a matter of time they gonna carry you out in a bag. Then all you good for is worms, and girl, that ain't gonna be clean.

No, you got to find a way, see miss, fill up your room. Make people want to come there with you. Need you. Make it so you wanna be there with your self, see. And it's some hard shit. Take everything you got make it worth-while. And sometimes, some certain moments, seem like it ain't worth how hard it is. And you gonna want to leave and take a ride and go fuck up your life again. Just don't seem to matter. What you gonna do then? What you got gonna hold you in your room when the moment tells you it ain't worth it? Girl, you got to have somethin' to love. And that may sound like some bad kinda poetry there, but hell, they got to base poems on somethin'. You got to have somethin'.

"I Hate Your Heart"

From *One Molecule*

Scene: The last moments between a couple that is separating, B leaving A.

A:

I hate your heart. It's so pliable. Or, what's that word? The science word – malleable! Who knew your heart would turn out to be so fucking malleable? We think we've got hold of steel here, something solid to build with! And then it just... melts into some-thing else. Conditions change. Molecules shift, rendering the material useless. Who knew such cold, hard permanence could be dissolved by something as soft as someone else's lips? You kissed someone. And now I have no taste for anything. Did you know, when you touched your lips to someone else's, that mine would go numb?

Or maybe you don't care for the question. You ask me one then. Do. Ask me one last question. Something that will hurt. But in a good way, to make me feel at least a little, the way it used to be, when you cared. Ask me a question that will make one of us sweat. Please. Ask something impossible that will let me die in the process, perish slowly on a thorn, that would be easier! Give me a task that is tangibly *fail-able!* So I could know what I lacked, or where I went wrong, or at least look at myself in the mirror to-morrow with some kind of repulsion that helps this make sense. Ask me something I can't answer, so I can sit benumbed and stupid in the silence. Don't leave me in the silence with my full faculties. That would be really mean.

"Bob Bean on Justice"

From *Ducks Crossing*

Scene: Bob Bean, a baffled philosophy professor, discourses to himself as he dresses to testify in a court case about which he is, as usual, uncertain.

BOB BEAN:

Well, ladies and gentlemen, today we go to court. And with good cause! With right on our side, and might! As in, one might be right. Or not. -- But most certainly in a practical sense, we are, if not in fact. For in truth, one might ask, "What is the true meaning of justice?" Would it be the allocation of an equitable reward or punishment? Or is it in fact the victory of right over might? Because then certainly we have the high road! Even when we know not where that high road goes.

In which case, my friends, we turn to the Old Testament, which tells us, "An eye for an eye and a tooth for a tooth." Yet the New Testament says, "Turn the other cheek" so, really, they sort of cancel each other out. But, I believe it was the Hebrews who had the more ancient wisdom. And it was a wizened old Rabbi who said, "Om shashana chom keir dullea." It is a beautiful language, is it not? Although obscure in meaning, and also the words. Anyway, Socrates, Socrates was a philosopher, and said of justice, many things! On the other hand he died a very unjust death, so can we really say he was impartial? Who knows?

For my own part, I, Bob Bean, must stand in behalf of community, and, friendship, and truth! And testify unto it! For where does the word 'testify' come from but the very word 'Testicle!' On which one swore in the old days, and told the truth, in a testicular posture, so as not to risk anything it is important not to lose... Which is not comforting.

Still... Still, one must attend, and stand forth! If for nothing else than because one has been subpoenaed. And, and, well let us note this!... The first three letters of the word 'Trial' are the same as in the word 'Triumph!' And *that* is the cornerstone upon which we base our testimony! Ha ha! Off we go!

(He exits, all dressed.)

"Conversation With God"

From *The Last Nickel*

Scene: Lonely & restless, Jo has invaded her sister's room at night and is keeping her awake, but really she is concerned about her sister's self destructive path since a death in the family.

JO:

I'm not trying to take over your life, I'm just having a hard time right now. Who am I supposed to turn to? God? God doesn't answer questions on how to deal with death. It's policy. He never answers *anything* directly, but, at least with other stuff it eventually becomes obvious. It unfolds, and you go, *"Oh! That's what that lesson was about! I get it, thank you!"* Or you get a sign. A flower blooms that never bloomed before, or a bird comes to you, or a Pez candy speaks. Something to give us a clue! But ask about death? "Um, God, about death?"   -

(as God)

"Sh! Can't talk about it!"

(As Self)

But, God? Hello? Are you listening?!

(God)

"What?! I gave you the 10 commandments, what do you want!"

(Self)

Well, I honor my mother and father & I don't pray to idols, how does this help me with the death thing?--"

(God)

"Look! You're just an individual, I'm omnipotent! I don't have time to deal with every little question you have, give it some thought, you'll figure it out!" Just think, think all the time.

(Looking at Jamie, meaning her)

Mull it over, carry it with you, take it to work, bring it home, stay up all night asking questions. Think 'till you're pale and you've got big rings under your eyes. Think 'till you're living on crackers and chocolate drink! If you think about it all the time, 'till you're *living* death & *breathing* death, maybe it'll make sense, because you'll be.. dead.

"Just Another Lump in the Ice"

From *Strange Grace*

Scene: Macy is a loner who may or may not have gone on a rampage. Stopping into an old roadside, the café owner has challenged the idea of violence.

MACY:

You know the funny thing? I never said I didn't have a gun.

(Macy pulls a semi-automatic.)

Seems like a powerful thing, doesn't it? Makes *you* nervous. Seems like it would even everything up. Except y'know, like you said, it *is* a load of horseshit. By the time you've bought it & loaded it & have it in your hand, you actually have less choice. And you'd think that would make things simple. But you've walked in with a gun & raised all the stakes to life and death, and that's way complicated. All of a sudden, everything matters. Who you choose to aim it at, and all the lives that effects. That's power. And nobody gets the power *not* to use it. You don't go in to blow your co-workers away & then just change your mind. You know why? Because that would be crazy. No, once you've got it, *it's* running the whole show. Congratulations, you just gave up your life to an inanimate object. Even now. I can't put it down because then you'd get it, and then you'd have no choice. Once you get that this snowball rolling, you become just another lump in the ice.

"Deberíamos Estar Abajo en el Cementerio"

From *Eating the Dead*

Special thanks to Johnny Sanchez and especially Alfonso Ramirez for their translation.

Scene: A garage in Mexico on the Day of the Dead. Reynaldo, a spiritualist with a checkered past, confronts the violent stranger Aphim.

REY:

Me recuerda de mi mismo. Tan furioso, como yo.

> *(To Aphim)*

Tienes una semilla dentro de tí, bien adentro de tu pecho. Como algo bien enroscadito, sí?

> *(Rey approaches him, growing dead serious, and for
> a moment we get a glimpse of a former Reynaldo.
> One who speaks with the sinister intimacy of one
> violent man to another.)*

Y lo que quieres es dejarlo ahí abajo, dejarlo bien enroscadito. Pero a veces lo sientes empujando contra tu pecho, a que no? Y quema. Y desearás que solo te duela, por que si algún día se explota y, se te escapa quemará a todo y destruirá a todos los que amas. Y tu rabia devorará al mundo.

> *(He opens his shirt, revealing the angry red marks
> of a primitive, probably prison-made tattoo: A
> snake eating the world.)*

Devorar al mundo.

> *(He steps blithely away, his intensity evaporating into
> regular, cheerful Rey.)*

No te preocupes no tienes que destruir nada. Para soltar la rabia solo tienes que soltar el mundo. Solo rinde el mundo! Hey, lo tengo!

> *(Rey pulls out a bag of candy : little sugar skulls and
> coffins.)*

Yo tengo el postre! Este es mi papá!

> *(He eats one.)*

Y esta es mi madre.

- continues -

REY: *(cont'd)*

(Eats another)

Y esta es Janis Joplin! Amigos, este es el Día De La Muerta! Y lo que sea para armar una buena fiesta!

(He jumps on a chair, opening the bottle he
brought for Jules, eating & drinking.)

(He jumps on a chair, opening the bottle he brought for Jules, eating Ahorita mismo, deberíamos estar abajo en el cementerio! Haciendo un pickinic. Y tomando como unos cosacos... Y celebrando como si nos fueramos a morir mañana! Porque, carnal, nunca se sabe? Hay que mostrar que todavía no estamos muertos! Cómete a los muertos! Y déjemos pasar nuestras penas! Y entonces alboreamos y amamos y peleamos y tomamos! Y rezamos... Rezamos de que estemos vivos lo suficiente.... para darnos cuenta que es lo que en verdad hace que valga la pena vivir. Eh?

(He steps down, breaking the spell.)

Thank you very much, five pesos por favor.

"We Should Be Down in the Graveyard"
From *Eating the Dead*

Scene: A garage in Mexico on the Day of the Dead. Reynaldo, a spiritualist with a checkered past, confronts the violent stranger Aphim.

REY:

He reminds me of me. So angry, just like me.

> *(To Aphim)*

You have a seed in you, deep in your chest. Like something coiled hard, right?

> *(Rey approaches him, growing dead serious, and for a moment we get a glimpse of a former Reynaldo. One who speaks with the sinister intimacy of one violent man to another.)*

And what you want is to keep it down there, keep it coiled tight. But sometimes it just pushes against your chest, doesn't it? And burns you. And you wish it would just go away, because if it ever escapes you it will burn everything and destroy everyone you love. And your rage will devour the world.

> *(He opens his shirt, revealing the angry red marks of a primitive, probably prison-made tattoo: A snake eating the world.)*

Devour the world.

> *(He steps blithely away, his intensity evaporating into regular, cheerful Rey.)*

Don't worry, you don't have to destroy anything. You just have to give up the world. Just give it up! Hey, I've got it!

> *(Rey pulls out a bag of candy : little sugar skulls and coffins.)*

I have dessert! This is my father!

> *(HE eats one.)*

And this is my mother.

> *(Eats another)*

- continues -

REY: *(cont'd)*

And this is Janis Joplin! Friends, it's the Day of the Dead! And anything for a good party, eh?

> *(He jumps on a chair, opening the bottle he brought*
> *for Jules, eating & drinking.)*

Right now we should be down in the graveyard! Having a picnic. And getting drunk. And partying like there's no tomorrow! Because who knows? We have to show we're still alive! Eat the dead! And digest our sorrows! Let us cuss and love and fight and drink! And pray... Pray that you keep alive long enough... to know what makes life worth living.

> *(He steps down, breaking the spell.)*

Thank you very much, five pesos please.

"Saved By A Moonbeam"

From *Nine*

Scene: Two women held against their will use mind games & stories to keep one another alive. Here 1 distracts 2 from intense pain.

1:

I fell in a pond once, at night, when I was really little, and it was so incredibly dark it was just black, and completely cold, and without breath and I was, really, I was drowning, because I could swim a little, but in the dark of this tomb you don't know which way is up! You just feel the water moving around you and you could be going down but you don't know! Because you don't know where the surface is, y'know? It was bad. And I was just frozen there, with no air and no hope and no idea which way was up! And then you know what happened?

This silver sliver nicked my eye and it made me turn my head, this little blinding flash, and I looked, and it was a moonbeam shining down through to me! Up through the water I saw the light spreading out and shimmering above me on the surface and I, I, I don't know how, I fought toward it, and I struggled up and went up, and with my last breath of life, I came up into the night air!

Isn't that something? I was saved by a moonbeam. I – I was saved. I was saved. By a moonbeam.

"Love is Like a Rare Bird"

From *The Destiny Thing*

Scene: *Meek broken-hearted Betty has witnessed the break-up of a young couple, now exhorts two strangers to action.*

BETTY:

Giuliana and Ernesto were in love. I mean really. I don't think true love is so common. And it would've been a problem if we hadn't shown up. And now they're in trouble! What if they never, ever get back together? Or worse?! I know that look they had. Terrible things can happen. And I think it would be immoral of us not to try and do something. To let love slip away, well, wouldn't that be a little like killing a mockingbird? Or at least something bad, involving a bird? Because love is, well, it *is* like a rare bird, and every-one who sees it, they each have their lives a little bit changed because of it. In a good way. Like a kind of a thing where we're all involved, and there's a thread, that connects us all? Around in a circle? A, a kind of circular destiny, but with the... bird thing, and maybe all of us have a responsibility to keep it going! Don't we?

"The Deeds Good Do-Bees Do"

From *Ducks Crossing*

Scene: Minnie, the fed-up proprietress of a run-down pool hall, makes one last repair as she tells her sister her plan.

MINNIE:

Hostetta, when we was growin' up, I was the restless one & you was the one scared to go 'round the block. 'Course that terrible mean dog with the big teeth lived 'round the block, but the point is, I wanted adventure & you didn't. An' I didn't say nothin' when I got stuck with this whole run-down, ramshackle, fallin'-apart & suckin'-the-life-outta-me pool hall, cause I'm not one to complain.

But Hoss, the time comes when ya gotta do what it is you was meant to do. I mean, providin' ya did all the stuff ya needed to get done in order to do that. *And* that ya know what it was you *wasn't* doin' that you was meant to. But I *do* know! And God knows I been a good do-bee. But I don't wanna end up *not* doin' what I should'a just cause I was busy doin' the deeds good do-bee's do. Ten years from now I just *gotta* be able to say, yes by golly, I did get done what I didn't back when I was doin' what I thought I oughtta, but really ought not'a, cause it wasn't what I was meant to! And Hoss, I think that makes it clear why I gotta go!

"I Got to Lay You Down"

From *Strange Grace*

Scene: Rendered slightly delirious after a breakdown, Bob has come to believe that the stranger
in his roadside café is the ghost of his brother Jim, who committed suicide when they
fought over a woman. Bob has realized he can never be reunited with that woman while
he remains haunted by his brother.

BOB:

I don't know how it is we come to this. We had all of life, God's hands
spreadin' it out like a banquet, the grief & glory, an' all the sugar & salt in
between. Ours to pick. And lookit us. Even a dog don't choose to starve.
How is it we come to do less?

Maybe ain't none of us is pure at heart, not with the best of intentions. Maybe that's what makes it so hard. I would'a never thought to choose against
ya. Even when we was fightin', I didn't never think it was a choice between
you & her. Even when I got the gun. I just thought to shock ya, make ya stop
hittin' her. Not to sever ya. But it does, is severs everything.

An' you ain't never left me, not for a day. How could I let ya go? You was my
brother. My only one. I gone clear to the half light with ya, bro. I am half
dead with keeping' you alive. But I am in that half of the light that leads to
wakin'. And you are in that half that leads to rest. An' I got to lay you down.

"Take a Pill or Something"

From *Commencing*

Scene: After Kelli's blind date turns out to be a lesbian, she also hits Kelli with a big overkill feminist rant. Kelli's response…

KELLI:

Man, that is a diatribe! Earth to person, lighten up! Take a pill or something. Look, I am not that much of a feminist or political or anything, okay? And, I'll be really frank with you, there is something seriously unattractive about a woman going off like that, okay? It's like, please don't foist your issues on me, alright, frankly? There's a lot wrong with the world but I'm not going to carry it all on my shoulders, I'm just trying to get through the fray one day at a time, one issue at a time, one crisis at a time! I never seem to have the nerve to say to people when they do this to me, please, I don't want to know about your beliefs! I'm not going to get sober, or change my life or fight the war, or save the, I dunnow, children-building-pandas-peasants or save the entire planet! Sorry. I just really have my hands full having a life, and a job and a few friends and making enough money and maybe even, God forbid, one day having a man in my life, and in my bed, please God, amen!

"Dropped & Bopped"
From *Subway*

Scene: Darcy, who has become sexually compulsive since the death of her partner, has just confessed the traumatic loss to one of her liaisons.

DARCY:

Yeah, I would rather be with her, wherever she is. In the great beyond. Except her ashes. Which are scattered. For the most part. I mean, I'm not holdin' onto 'em or anything but... Well anyway, not important. Just, y'know. She had it in her will to be scattered off the Coney Island Pier. So, you do that. I mean you try. It's just, they were, y'know, she was, in this can thing and – we really don't have to get into this if you don't want to. It's just, the subway was coming, and I, my hands were shaking and I kinda.. dropped her. And the can broke open. And she started getting all over the platform and, blowing, onto the tracks.

> *(Suddenly tempted to laugh at the absurd horror of it.)*

It's so stupid! I've actually been too afraid to tell anyone that, because it's so fuckin' stupid! All these people were stepping on her, and I was trying to scoop her up, and completely losing it... And then this woman came along and tried to help me, and, took me for a drink to calm me down, and...I kinda ended up bopping her in an alley outside the Puck Building.

I mean, I dunnow know what to say! She was supposed to get released into the ocean. And instead I kinda... well... dropped & bopped.

"You Will Feel the Breeze"

From *The Destiny Thing*

Scene: *Spike, a dead 80's punk rocker who is the guardian angel of the Brooklyn Bridge, is must compel Jerry, an emotionally stunted scammer, to help repair a glitch in destiny.*

SPIKE:

I dunnow why you wanna make this hard on yourself! It ain't like we're on different sides! But really, it is not seemly to question an angel's motives. Your little earth-bound minds are *so slow,* what does it take to get you to open your eyes? You think one thing can happen that doesn't effect everything else? You think you can cheat all your life and not – It's *all connected*, Jerry, get on the web! And I don't mean the internet! Your ethernet is a primitive metaphor, get it? A butterfly flaps it's wings in Brazil, you will feel the breeze. But if that insect doesn't fly, Jerry, what if it never learns to fly? You never loved! Yes, I fell from grace, but at least I loved! All of them, every soul who comes who comes to the bridge, you see them, you watch with a sort of nostalgia that makes your heart ache for every one. You don't know what it's like, to look into the faces of strangers and know their hearts. The agony and emptiness and chatter and…abject loneliness. Feeling it is… penance. For a life mislived. And your penance, meaty boy, is helping me.

"A Wonderful Emptiness"

From *HellEden*

Scene: *A numb group of soldiers has formed a tribe and gone primal. As their humanity reawakens, so does the world around them.*

FLETCH:

I saw her! I just saw her! Oh, God! My heart feels...

(Points to his chest)

Look! It's thumping. You know, her, from before? Moving through the wood! I turned, and she was standing there, looking right at me! Smiling! I saw her teeth. They were white. I wonder what she eats. I just stood there, it felt, I dunnow, like my heart was gonna just fly off up into the air! And she lifted her hand to me! – Oh, plumbs, good, I'm hungry. – But I'm not. It's so weird! ...

She's out there.   And I might see her again. I mean, she's not one of us. She's not...tribe. But.. it's like I've always missed her. How can that be? I've never even touched her and now, it's like I'm cold without her. And it's not lonely either, but it is. And it's not pain, but it's like an ache. I have an emptiness now, and it's wonderful.

"Someplace in Mexico"

From *Eating the Dead*

Scene: *Aphim, an abusive American dealer, has chased his kleptomaniac girlfriend all the way to Mexico to get his drugs back. She's not there, and now he is stuck holding a Mexican local hostage who doesn't speak English.*

APHIM:

Man, I am so lost I can't find my ass! I just... I don't know where I am, I don't even know how I got here. And I don't mean just literally, savvy? Last month I had money & love & business is good & everything's copasetic. And now, all of a sudden I'm standing in a, craphole, someplace in Mexico, watching this idiotic stranger – and I don't mean you, I mean me – gesticulating, and speaking in foreign tongues, and threatening people! And I'm such a nice guy, I really am!

You don't even know what I'm talkin' about, do you? I'm a lost man in an alien world. And I don't think that's gonna change when I go home. Some-how you just go along, same as always, building what you can build, and then one day you walk around a corner and *Bam!* Suddenly you're a foreigner in your own life. How does that shit happen? Huh?

Well, maybe it's just the nature of life, huh? We cycle around, things change. They say every seven years the molecules you're made up of are all com-pletely new. But, man. It's like, I don't know the currency, I can't read the signs, and I have no idea which direction leads to home.

"Sex in a Bar Bathroom"

From *Commencing*

Scene: Having been set up on a disastrous blind date with a straight woman, recovered alcoholic Arlin made the mistake of confessing an indiscretion, which is now being bandied about by her "date", who's getting drunk.

ARLIN:

I suppose sex in a bar bathroom does sound sexy. The reality is that you both stink like cigarettes & booze, and don't know what the other person likes, and you're trying to stand up, and breathing in the smell of urine & farts & those cheap air fresheners, and neither of you wants to get on the germy floor or get your clothes wet. And you do something totally intimate with an absolute stranger, and when you're done, you haven't become more intimate with her, you're just, more of a stranger to yourself.

God knows drinking really adds to it. That feeling of being an alien in the world. That you're marooned on a planet where the gravity doesn't fit you. And everybody else is nicely grounded, and you try to fit in, but you're always lumbering around, pulled down by everything around you, or else you're hovering just above, too lightweight to even register. Trying to make conversation while you're in imminent danger of drifting away. At the first careless remark, you'll get blown off into space to float alone forever. And sometimes we almost wish it would go ahead & happen, so you can at least have the quiet of floating in the cold dark. And the main thing is, the one thing you know for sure, is that the drinking is *not* the problem.

"Small Blue Marble"
From *Gencybo*

Scene: When an astronaut discovers that her mission was really to dump nuclear waste in space, she refuses to complete the mission. With her crew locked out in the cargo bay, her transmission time to earth dwindles.

CAPTAIN HAIMER:

We knew we were not fully informed when we undertook this mission. We knew we were sponsored by a corporation that endorsed nuclear power. We were aware that some materials on board were related to that. The price of the ride was not asking. But we were told this mission carried telecommunications equipment. I am an honorable officer. I have discharged my duties faithfully. But I am looking at the planet earth right now. And my hand will not serve to release 50 tons of nuclear waste around it.

KTLK, can you still hear me? I'm still transmitting. We don't know what the result of dumping nuclear waste would be. Not one of you back at home can tell me. We don't even know what it's doing to our own planet. Maybe it'll just float off, I'm sure that's the plan. But it wasn't the mission.

I know you can hear me back there, Bill. I know the crew is getting cold. You were right, what you said, not everything in life is our responsibility. Just the things we can control. I won't be readmitting you to the ship. I know you would try and stop me. But this ship isn't going home.

I can still see you, back on earth. Do you know what you look like? A marble. A small blue marble. My daughter's there. – Hello, transmitting. We're losing transmission, do you read?... If you can still hear me, I want you to do me a favor. Buy me a marble. When we're gone, a blue marble. Someday, I want you to give it to my daughter. Put it in her hand. And tell her for me. She can handle it.

"Different Kinds of Brains"

From *The Idiot's Guide to the Brain*

Scene: *The Lecturer, who narrates a talk with the audience on the nature of brains, has explained left and right brains, said to be our analytical and creative sides, using as examples the Lecturer, learning-disabled but hyper-creative, and the Lecturer's father, a scientist.*

LECTURER:

I guess my dad & I just had different kinds of brains. He was a left-brain kinda guy & I was a right-brainer. His language was one of nature theory and historical analysis. And mine, an intuitive language of emotional expression. We never could seem to cross that bridge to one another's minds. We could wave from the other side. It was many years before I understood that we simply had different kinds of intelligence.

In the last few days of his life my dad was very ill, and eventually slipped into a kind of dementia. He kept trying to get up, and when we asked him why, he said, "Because I have to complete the fusion." I asked him if one of us could do 'the fusion' for him. But he said, "No, I'm the only one who knows how to render the materials malleable."

I know that whatever he meant by 'The Fusion' had to do with the science still running in his head. Or maybe it was about the Big Fusion. Y'know, leaving your body and becoming one with the cosmos. But, for me, it's also a beautiful metaphor for the Right/Left Brain conundrum. Everyone has to achieve their own Fusion between the Creative & the Analytical. It's up to each of us to find our own unique blend.

"No Purpose at All"

From *The Gentlemen of Grammercy Park*

Scene: *Victorian era, New York City. A lady's weekly hobby club has begun to crack the veneer of formality and form deeper friendships. Here the cheery hostess takes confidence in one of the members.*

LUCINDA:

Voltaire and Blake! Dear, how dreary! And nothing but the bare trees for company. If I suffer for purpose, you at least do not. It is my comfort, your budding family and your womanly grace, why God's purpose is evident in every step you take. Ah! If I could feel for a *moment* even a degree of such clarity!

But nevermind me. It's a bad humour taken me today. A pretty thing, is it not? A maudlin old spinster, moping about. But God, I shall be 28 in February! And alone in this world much the sooner. Here I shall be, ensconced in this tomb with my shoddy riches and morose heart, a giddy biddy. – No, you needn't protect my feelings, I know how people laugh at me. It is difficult to stay abreast of the times when one has been raised in the glue of antiquity.

My father has been dying for 13 years, and how selfishly I dreamed of the day when Lucinda Bonnemaker would at last be turned loose, to spring into the full blood of her life! And now the time is actually near, I find I live in dread. Soon I shall be forced to awaken and see that Lucinda Bonnemaker has no purpose at all.

"The Course a Love"

From *Ducks Crossing*

Scene: *A wedding party in the Parthanon Pool Hall, Lemming Colorado. The owner's cranky sister Hostetta is pressed to make a toast to love.*

HOSTETTA:

They say the course a love never did run smooth. That's why ya gotta squash it. Now by that I don't mean it can't take place, for loveth is.. divinith and, so forth. It just works better packed in a *small* box. And is therefore contained, givin' it somethin' to squooze out of. For the quality of love is to squooze, and therefore not overwhelm its recipient. For love is a thing of discretion! And it can be kinda ooey-gooey, but not that ooey-gooey sickie-sweetie snickie-doodle kinda thing, that just makes everyone around you wanna barf. And don't just glomp love down either! 'Cause that's just stupid. Ya gotta test it! Like, y'know, give it a good whack to see if it comes back. An' if it does, well, then ya know ya got a good, comin'-back kinda thing, that's oozy but not sickie, & comes back when ya whack it, and is like a turtle dove! Yeah. Like a... white... frilly kinda turtle dove that just... Ah, the hell with it, if ya don't know what love is already yer a idiot 'cause ya just got married, cheers!

"Helldevil"

From *Reap the Wild Historian*

Scene: Casey, a super chipper young lesbian 'herstory' student, has been interviewing a salty old dyke about the early gay rights movement, putting a shiny spin on it. The elderly activist has demonstrated resistance by obstinately resisting the interview. Finally Casey snaps...

CASEY:

Oh, for God's sake – Helldevil, what is it you want? What do you want from me? What does it take to do a simple video interview? Would you like me to beg? Do you wanna see me cry, on the floor, with my head up my ass? Just tell me, Bertha. Because I'll do it. Big Bertha, Earth-Mother-Dyke-Goddess to all us little miniature everyday lesbians, do you want me to throw up my everyday lesbian barf, because that's what I want to do. God, I so do not deserve this. All I wanted was to turn in my little project and graduate. And maybe win a couple competitions & go to Sundance & possibly have a career. But no. I'll just cut my little dyke wrists, and then my parents can gloat. They were right, I *should* have studied business & married Mark McGuire. Thank you, History Legend! Thank you for making everything so clear. Now I can go home and finish moving out! And *Haley* can go on shtupping undergrads!

(Remembers audience.)

And we have an audience! That's so great! They can share your advise about constipation, and maybe it'll stop my dog from shitting all over the apartment, which I'm sure he's doing right now! God, it's good to talk to old people! You're so VERY VERY VERY HELPFUL! AND NOW I'M HYPER-VENTILATING!

"Batman"

From *The Good Drum*

Scene: A convict is addressing those who will witness his execution.

EDDIE:

Then last of all, I don't have anything much, but there are these comics that I had in jail, that Mr. Lispenard is holding. I am leaving them in my will to Kenny Alter. I am not sure that he will want them. They are almost all Bat-man. I think they are good, especially the art. But Mr. Alter may not take them, in light of my killing his wife. I killed her with a gun and my hands, but comic books is all I have.

Mr. Alter is who pushed for this situation, so I guess it will be better after I am dead. Because he has had a bad shock. I don't feel sorry for him, because I am a sociopath and they tell me I don't know how it feels for other people.

But I think maybe the media is a sociopath too, because they don't seem to know how other people feel either. Because they print all those things and had that show on, showing her body, and that must have made Mr. Alter feel bad, I don't know, but they also put that stuff in about how I am the "Point Blank Murderer." I did not expect to become one of the bad guys. When I read comic books, I always thought in terms of being the hero, and saving people. There wasn't a lot of people to save in Olaire. I didn't really save *anybody*. I didn't find anybody to save. But I always thought more like Batman. So I don't know how it ended up this way.

If anybody here needed a good job done, I would be a good person to ask! I have a heart beating inside me, just like you. And I'm not saying don't kill me, but I'm like the drum, the good Indian drum in Eagle Scouts? Where somebody keeps the rhythm and everybody else does something to it, like a war cry or oath, but one person keeps the beat, and that's the beating of goodness, and my heart's like that! And once, I pulled a dog out of the mud!

"The Nameless Lips"

From *Subway*

Scene: When Darcy's anonymous sexual encounter won't stay anonymous, she would rather leave than have her heart awakened.

DARCY:

Don't ask me my name, forget me! Goddamit! You're breaking my heart and I don't have any heart left! I gotta go.

(Grabs her gym bag & starts to leave.)

I'm supposed to walk away and leave you, where the hell am I supposed go? I'm not going home, I can't go to work. I can go to bars & have sex, that I could do, plain & simple, and preferably lurid, and goddamn you for wrecking that. Why did you have to foist your life on me? I was doing very well as a shell. I don't need you to come in here and wake things up, I can't do it. Why can't you just stay anonymous? That's what anonymous sex is, the drinks & sweat & the nameless lips & the nothing. I have no compassion for you. If you were stupid enough to stay alive then my condolences, I don't want it. I don't even know what I'm doing here, I'm supposed to be with her! We did everything else together, the chemo & the radiation & the diet, and I dutifully pushed pills down her throat & took her to the hospital & stuck her with needles, and we were supposed to do it together! I don't know what kind of a world it is that she's gone and I'm still here. And I don't understand. You're the Christian, is this punishment?

"The Planet Jupiter"

From *The Last Nickel*

Scene: Banished to a corner of her sister's room, Jo finds a way to talk about loneliness.

JO:

The planet Jupiter is 40 million miles away. They talk about visiting other planets, but it's *40 million miles*. If we sent someone right now, they wouldn't even *arrive* until 2,038. And for them to get back, it would take until they were 90 years old. If they ever got back at all.

And when he got there, what would he find? Signs of previous life, little bacteria fossils, but not necessarily people. We've never seen signs of anything even remotely like life. Maybe in some other galaxy, but not here. Do you know what that means? It means this is it. As far as finding companionship, you can forget it. There are no neighboring party planets, we're not gonna find company any time soon. Maybe ever. We're it. The singular little island surrounded by space & vacant bodies. The only oasis with conscious life, floating around, with just enough awareness to know how alone we are. Don't you think that's scary?

"It's All Absurd"

From *The Gentlemen of Grammercy Park*

Scene: Victorian New York. Gossiping among her circle of friends, the highly marriageable
Angelina explains how she hopes to avoid a forced match by spending all her time Kirby,
a witty fop.

ANGELINE:

Me? Serious on Kirby Baker? How completely absurd. You can't be serious
on someone who doesn't even take himself seriously. Which is precisely
what I like about him. I'm sick to death of the others! Always sniffing around,
every one of them taking *great* pains to extol his modesty to me, while seizing
absolutely every opportunity to flaunt his worth! It's utterly absurd. All the
posturing, and prostrating, and protesting with heart-strung voice. And then
dashing off for a nip & peck as soon as they're out the door. It wouldn't be
near so boring if they'd at least admit it. Now *that* might be interesting!
Wouldn't it be divine if he could say, "I'm utterly putting on airs in order to
marry you, and later I'll be visiting a house of ill repute!" And *I* could reply,
"Why thank you, I have no interest in marrying anyone at any point in time,
but do lets hear about the brothel!" As it is, we shall all go right on
pretending. And sooner or later the butterfly shall be netted and pinned. In
the mean, I thank God for the occasional decadence, and a man who can
laugh at himself.

"Two Little Ganoods"

From *Eating the Dead*

Scene: Jilted, betrayed and ripped off by his girlfriend Shay, Aphim has chased her all the way to Mexico, just to discover she has a lover there, and to top if off, it's a woman.

APHIM:

I may be runnin' hot, honey, but I don't need a plan. I'm goin' on instinct. Basic instinct. A man has his pride. And a smidgen of dignity to walk this earth with. When a woman makes a fool out of that, she abuses her God-given power. And Shay did it with relish! Women hold the power of life and death right in their loins. It behooves you to be a little nice. What do men have? Two little ganoods with which to run around and spread a little seed. Sometimes it takes, sometimes it doesn't. You tell me who's got the advantage. You tell me, considering that outrageous imbalance, whether the male of the species can be forgiven for making sure his little nuggets get the credit and dignity they're due. And if we overreact once in a while when we're made a total asshole out of, maybe it's because we can ill afford to let one of those ganoods get whacked off. So do me a favor, don't advise me! Just be pleasant!

"I Want You to Pilot"

From *Glass Jaw*

Scene: The emotionally unstable Arthur attempts to help his social worker Jeff understand the power of the imaginary worlds that he & his sister travel. He has convinced Jeff to sit by him in a chair, each holding a golf club as a piloting stick.

ARTHUR:

(Looking out front, as if out the front of the space ship.)

An asteroid field is usually about the size of a football field. The movies always show the whole field, but it's not really like that. There's no light in space. It's more like one of those submersibles. Only what you can see in the headlights. Basically, you're the Titanic and everything else is icebergs.

(Sees Jeff's doubt.)

I know, I understand what you're thinking. If this was just about sitting here with a stupid golf club in my hand, you think I'd bother? I want you to know how to fly. No, I want you to know how to pilot, but I can't do it for you, *I* can't mess with your head, *you* have to. Because it's in there. All of space. Your universe, more detailed & infinite than anything you've ever seen!

Close your eyes. You have to feel it. Concentrate. The ship pulls. It wants to drift. If you let it, it will float until you die. There are gravitational pulls that you don't understand yet, but you can learn to feel them. Put all your focus and all your faith here. Don't *do* anything, don't project anything, just listen with your hand. The chaos is out there. Your whole life can spin away. But you have the power to exert your will. And if you can't feel that, you will never pilot anything.

"Masks"

From *The Gentlemen of Grammercy Park*

Scene: Victorian era New York. The Compte D'Liissard, a slick Frenchman of false royal claim, has discovered a woman masquerading as a man in the gentleman's club he frequents.

COMPTE D'LISSARD:

I am not one to begrudge a good disguise. In fact, I have admiration for this. But, one must beware what one gets from the deceit. Some faces you assume and, no matter is false, the effect is authentic. In this one may discover something real of one's self. But some, the disguise is not for the benefit of others, but to hide from yourself. This is I think not so wise. Once you are letting it go, this true face is not so easy to find again. In the end, who will you be? Mm? Of this I know something. Perhaps one day you will visit me at my apartments and we will explore it thoroughly.

"I Remember What it is To Be Close"

From *Strange Grace*

Scene: *It has just been implied that loner Macy is insensitive to people because it's been so long since she's been close with anyone.*

MACY:

I haven't forgotten what it is to be close. I remember it. All the time. I remember it more vividly than people who actually have it. I can close my eyes and feel skin tone and texture. I can smell sweat just by thinking about it. Women's sweat smells like chicken soup. If you've never slept with a woman you probably don't know that. The tiny way an errant piece of armpit hair curls forward into that little crease in the front of the arm. The way someone's hair falls on a pillow. Curly hair sits, always a little bit alert. Straight hair slides down the front of the pillow. Wavy hair cascades. That's my favorite. Best of both worlds. Wild, full of promise, but acquiescing too, open to receiving you. The way it feels to slide into bed together naked, skin to skin, before you're sweaty, just cool silk curtains blowing against one another. How someone's lips demand all your faculties, and we have to close our eyes, because all our concentration has gone to those lips, for just that moment, so you do not miss the smoothness, or the mild scent of rose, or the gentle intake of breath. I can remember a soft, sliding caress more acutely than when someone's hand was actually on my thigh. I'm sorry, am I distracting you?

"The Bone Counter"

From *Eating the Dead*

Scene: Knowing that Brea is still angry with her, Shay now seeks to regain her favor by telling this story. Shay's stories always succeed, and often seduce, because they are fiction but have a strange kind of truth.

SHAY:

Can I just talk to you while you're painting? I just... I've been on the road for five days, driving alone, and I'm lonely for talk really.

I went by chariot as far as the river Nile. When I got to Thebes, I went to see a bone-counter that my sisters at the boreum recommended. She was an old hag, and the bones she counted came from a cord around her neck. Human bones. And it gave me a chill You don't know, at times like that, if it's something bad, or just the ethereal raising the electricity all around you. She threw the bones and said, 'You're going to finally find your tribe. For the first time in your life, you will belong. And that's the good news.'

'And what's the bad news then, old goat mother?' I asked her. 'Well,' she said, 'They're a cannibal tribe.' 'Are you telling me, that I belong to a tribe of flesh eaters?! Because that's evil, I will never eat people!'

'Your tribe,' she said, 'do not eat one another. You each devour yourself.' She said this as the river rolled by and the sun shown down. That every one of my ancestors had done it before me. Each bit and chewed and swallowed themselves. 'And in this way,' she says, 'each one digested herself, and excreted herself, and fell into the earth, and came up out of the earth a growing self, with greens, and purple for branches, Brea, and leaves for hair, stretching from the clay and blossoming herself and saying, "OH GOD-DESS! I AM MADE IN MY OWN IMAGE!"

"Thermometer of Thrills"

From *A Rage of Chaos*

Scene: A gay man returns to the weekend retreat he once frequented with his circle of friends, the sole AIDS survivor among them. He has been trying not talk about the past, and here we come to understand the dilemma it presents.

MAN:

God help the bumpkin that decides to see what's in this vase! Eight and a half years' worth of chicken gristle, chewed gum, cigarette ash and roach butts! Ham used to come down and smell it in the morning to gage how much of a good time we'd had the night before. This was helpful when you couldn't quite remember yourself. 'Thermometer of Thrills'.

(Demonstrating, he smells it)

"Ah. 8.5: moderate blow out."

(Smells it)

Ew. Straight 9: serious fun, late night."

(Smells it)

"Aach! That's putrid! We had *so* much fun! 10's across the board!"

So, that's another one of those things. It has significance. Every-thing has a connotation. Meaning. The longer you live, or the more people that die, the more things and places take on a connotation. So little is just what it is, everything has a memory tied up in it al-ready, because somebody did something once, made it a Thrill Thermometer or whatever, so that something just even similar is going to remind you, and now *it* has meaning!

And the first person you ever know that dies, you want to keep his things forever, all of them, the pictures and the records and the knickknacks, because it reminds you of him and he meant some-thing to you, and if he's really gone forever, by God, you can stave off mortality for him in this way, just a little bit of him, show a little bit of loyalty by holding his knick-knacks above the tide: I *wear* his shirts, I *knew* him!

And the same with somebody else you knew that died, and for the second and third people who get sick, whether you knew them well, they were members of the flock, you owe 'em, so you use the lamp. It signifies.

And if you lose a number of people over the years, you begin to take less and reject more. You resent it. These things, these mementos, take on a weight of their own, making so much of your life too laden to use! Until you can't

- continues -

MAN: *(cont'd)...*

remember anymore... where the glass came from... Surely you have some sense of what I'm talking about, of wanting something of someone's because this was that person, you knew them now they're gone but it's... got... fingerprints... There's a presence of death. The.. fingerprints of dread, on the glass itself like plague, and it can give it to you, and you never want to touch anything again. But if you don't, you'll die.

"Something Divine"

From *Three to Get Ready*

Scene: Moira is an agoraphobic who has become closely involved with her neighbor Lo. It is only after Moira has betrayed Lo that she realizes how important her neighbor has become. Now Moira must find a way to express that, even if it means going outside and talking to Lo through the bars on Lo's apartment window.

MOIRA:

What happens to a person, that's not what defines them, you know? Lo? Or what mistakes they make. I thought for a long time I was just the woman who got hit. And, maybe deserved it. But I don't believe that anymore. And I swear, as sure as I'm standing out here on this ledge, I know you didn't hurt Lanie! I know I – that I've cost you something I ever make up, and I should have believed you, but I didn't – I just – I was scared... No, you know, really, what I was, was faithless. But I'm not now. I don't care whether anything makes any sense, it doesn't have to. Because I think maybe we are the sense, Lo. We're the sense, and the light, and the great art, and the open highway, and the bits & pieces! And you don't have to let me in if you can't, but you gave that to me! And I think that is something divine, whether you believe in that kind of thing or not. Not believing doesn't make it not true. I know I can't take back what I did. But I can't go away either. And not just because I don't know how to get down off this ledge. I have to pee really bad too. So would you open this gate and let me in?

"This is How We Did it"

From Reap the Wild Historian

Scene: Bertha, a senior dyke, is being interviewed for a documentary on the history of gay activism. Repelled by the spin put on the interview, Bertha has practiced resistance on the interview itself, until the Interviewer finally dropped the shine and had a fit. Now Bertha can address her genuinely.

BERTHA:

This is how we did it. How we made change. The whole social revolution thing, exactly like I been doin' to you. By bein' one big stubborn pain in the ass. And like you just did. By screaming. And shouting, and losing our cool, and failing and doubting ourselves, and hating history, and disappointing our parents, and railing against unfair shit-heads like me. That's how change happens. Some of it's noble. And there's always heroism. But most of the time it's nothing more than being so completely frustrated that you become willing to lose yourself & throw a big fat shitty hissy right in the middle of the room. The spit & shine, that all comes later. When the hard shit is done. And I got news for ya. You ain't missed a thing. Cause it ain't over. There's a lot to do. And if you wanna make any difference, you better get busy. 'Cause it's your neighborhood now, cowboy.

"Every Wavelength Has its Limits"

From *Gencybo*

Scene: Glib talk show host Doug has largely made fun of his live radio interview with astronauts in space. Until its captain announces that she is sacrificing herself & the lives of her crew rather than complete a mission to dump nuclear waste in space. All appeals from command have now failed and transmission is growing weak.

DOUG:

Hey... Peg? Doug here. Can you read me?... Listen, you, you knew the gig, right? And, y'know, it's a big universe. You can't come back with the cargo, so why don't you just dump it? I mean, God knows you don't wanna lose your crew, right? -- Well, God, I don't know about God, I don't think he gets late-night radio, and if he does, I don't guess he's my biggest fan, right? Fortunately, I think, every wavelength has its limits. Listen, I'm... I'm just a vulgar ass on late night radio. But you, you got a crew that's freezin' to death up there, and a lotta reasons to come back, and maybe everything doesn't require an act of conscience! Okay? It's an imperfect world! I admire you don't wanna make it worse. But you're gonna die up there. And I just, can't seem to square that with the whole shitty little vulgar rat race we got runnin' around on the majority of this planet. Nobody else is killin' themselves over it! Not your bosses at cent-com, not the pea-heads listening to this show, all three of 'em, and *certainly* not me! Why does it have to be you?! Why do the people who still have a shred of integrity have to do the decent thing when the rest of us go on spewing bloat & talking out our ears & thinking that's funny?! Alright? It's just... I really can't fathom... how you square that.

"I Stood For Love"

From *Strange Grace"*

Scene: When Macy enters a café intent on killing herself there, she reawakens a past trauma for the proprietor & his lover. As Macy's concern for them grows, it becomes increasingly hard to reconcile their love with the loss of her own.

MACY:

I don't want myself back, that's not what happens when you love! You don't get to ask for it back. You're not just tossing out some free ends you can spare. If you really truly love somebody, you give them the best, grade-A, spare no expense. Center of the bullseye. And if somebody's brave enough to reach out, you damn well better ante up the best part of yourself. The innermost tender seed. And if you really mean it, it's not a risk, it's a privilege.

You don't get to send your heart out everyday. Our hearts beat every minute of our whole lives in the dark cavern of our bodies. Once in your life, maybe twice if you're lucky, it crosses over to somebody else, in some unfathomable way, to some unseeable light. And maybe that's faith, because you're never gonna see it or have any proof. You just have to take the blind bet on that feeling, that unseeable lightness. I don't know if there's a God, but that's about as close to divinity as I expect to get.

And I don't know any other way to do it. If giving yourself is the cost, then I'm glad to have paid. I'd pay it again if I had it. I stood for love. If hers was fleeting, mine was not. Even if my seed is the only one in the pot. I stood for love.

"I Let Go"

From *Prelude to Walking*

Scene: When an angel comes to take a dead soldier from the earth, he refuses to go, trying instead to reacquaint her with the beauty of being alive.

HERSHAL:

But there's more, you understand, than just the big life things. There's the small, that lets you know it's worth being alive. There's taste, like coffee, and like jam! And the rain, on your face, and it makes you wet and uncomfortable, but at the same time it makes you a part of everything? And that, that rusty orange in the sunset sometimes, you remember? A searing rose color that you see it, and it's so good it aches?

(Indicates the dead bodies on the ground.)

Even them. Even this.…is worth more than nothing. Even the charred flesh and curled fingers… The way their teeth show now, but you should have seen them when they laughed! Not one I wouldn't sit in the dirt with & laugh again. Even when the dirt turned to mud, and our feet rotted. And we heard those first sounds. How we looked at one another… Wasn't one didn't look their mother's child then. When the noise overtook us. And the fire. And the rain. There was vigor in their hearts and vigor in the action… but the faces all looked startled how our bodies broke like plates. And we screamed without knowing. This one cried like a baby, and no longer smiled. He just bled.

What I knew when I held him, was not the screaming or the crying, or the shattering of plates, or the trees catching fire… but the look in his eyes, like a child wanting home, before it stopped making sense and somehow have it all again, And you want to grab the pleading face and cry the futility of going back, or going on, or anything at all, the whole jagged pointless world, especially the good parts, because none of it lasts! There was nothing I could say in those final moments, to explain why the sound of a cricket should have mattered. And the blood, all the blood, it pours out like it matters, but it just dries up like rain. And the trees all burned, not a leaf of them left, not a place for a single leaf to be. When the rain, and the leaves, and the crickets were all gone… I let go, didn't I?

"Shitty, Painful & Bitter"

From *Friends of the Deceased*

Scene: *In a graveyard, a widow has offered a young runaway, Lanie, money to tell a shitty story about her dead husband, so she won't miss him. Within the fiction of Lanie's story, she ends up telling the truth.*

LANIE:

(Lanie paces, tossing the story out cavalierly.)

Okay, shitty, painful & bitter, that's what you want? It's your money. Okay so, I was this total freak at home, right? So I ran away a couple weeks ago. And I hitchhiked all the way here. And couple nights ago, this guy stopped & offered me a ride. He seemed really nice. And it was Gerald. Yeah. Really. He was a really nice guy, right? He even bought me some McDonald's. And I was thinkin', wow, this is gonna work out, I'm gonna do okay. And then when we got here, instead of dropping me at my friend's, he pulls over in this, like, warehouse parking lot . And of course he asks if he can feel me up.

(Doing her best to remain indifferent.)

And, I was so stupid, I thought if I just talked to him like a person, he would understand, 'cause he's this really nice guy, y'know? So I tell him, like, I'm not into that, that I'm saving myself for marriage. And it was like I set off a bomb, he just turns into this total freak right in the car! And he started – No, you'll like this, this is the painful part! He started grabbing me all over me, and he got over on my side of the car and he... then he... ... hurt me.

(Lanie stares off. Tries to summon her bravado, but it's pale.)

Horrible enough for you? Good. Then I'll just finish. Afterwards he let me out of the car and left me there. But it was like, part of me never got out of the car. I don't think he meant to. But he drove off with this murdered kid. And... I just didn't know that could happen. That a part of you could die. ... Maybe later he left her by a dumpster. And somebody found the body and took it to a morgue. They never will know who she was. So they buried her in an unmarked grave. The dirt is still fresh. So I came to mourn her.

"Lesbian-ish"

From *Subway*

Scene: Alice has undertaken a late-night tryst with another woman, but finds it difficult not to feel guilty about her husband.

ALICE:

Look, I don't want to talk about Alan! Why are you so obsessed with Alan, Alan is fine! You don't want to talk about yourself, well forget I ever mentioned Alan! He's a, a blank, okay?! For the rest of the night, as far as you're concerned, I am just a single, anonymous, sex-crazed, lesbian-ish sex person! Semi-lesbian! Semi-bi! Semi-sexual bifocal -- I don't know what it is, you figure it out! And when you do, go explain it to Alan, because he's certainly trying to understand! And I can't think of a single thing to tell him this time.

You can say, "Oh, I'm late, I ran into an old friend," and he'll understand. You can explain that you had to double-up at the conference and that's why a strange woman is answering the phone in your hotel room, and he'll accept that. He knows it's not true, he's not stupid, but he doesn't want to push you. He puts your needs before his own, that's the kind of person he is. He just wants you to be okay.

What can I possibly say to explain coming home at 4 a.m.? "Sorry honey, I know it's dawn but I had a *real bad* flat tire"? There is nothing I can tell him to make it make sense! Because it doesn't. I don't understand me at all. Why would you do this to someone you love? I have everything I need and I am not okay.

"Keg-o-rama"
From *Colter's Last Stand*

Scene: While their plans for world domination go awry, Colter reports on the afternoon's progress.

COLTER: *(on cell)*

Hey, dude, we got it! ... Totally, yeah! 24 gallon. Keg-o-rama! I'm stoked! ... I know, it's gonna be awesome. And guess what? They didn't even card me.... Yeah, you owe me ten bucks. ... Dude, you're so lame, *you* said they would, *I* said they wouldn't! Anyway, I'm done with your car. .... Yeah, no, it's in a lot. We're not back at the dorm yet, you wanna pick it up? ... Great. Oh, and can you bring 200 bucks?... We need bail. ... Yeah. ... No, dude, I told you, we got the keg, no problem. .... Ah, it was this thing with a cop. Duber hit him.... The guy just wouldn't stop askin' questions, y'know? It's like, don't put The Dube on the spot.. But this guy was just goin' on, "Oh, we have to do a report." ... Oh, this car accident.... No, us, we hit a tree. ... Dude... D... Dude, easy off, okay?! Your car's okay, it's just the bumper!... Nah, a few dents, we'll pound 'em out. It's not even like it was Duber's fault, y'know? His sleeve was on fire. ... Yeah, it's like, he's tryin' to put out this massive fire in the back seat & his sleeve caught & it distracted him. And the other cars are like, 'scuse me, could you possibly swerve *away* from our car, not *toward* us?! It was crazy! Cars are screetchin' & pilin' up all around us and it's like, damn man, watch *out,* we just bought this keg!

Jane Shepard

"She's Got the Name"

From *Nine*

Scene: Chained in a basement and abused, two women struggle to keep one another alive. When 2 suffers unbearable pain from an internal injury, the other prisoner distracts her by demanding to know her name. It works, as 2 rises out of pain with this response.

2:

You can't have my name! You'll never have it! You can shoot me or cut me or fuck me to death or whatever it is they'll do, I don't give a shit! That'll be the end of this shell and thank God for worms & maggots. But nobody will have killed me because *I* was never here! This room never heard my name. The first time they did those things to me, it wasn't me anymore. I am not the kind of person this happens to. And what you see here, isn't me. It, it ripped out of my body and flew away, *shuuu*! Far away! She's gone! Free. She's got the name. And they've got *nothing*.

"Down Deep Where the Serpents Roll"

From *Glass Jaw*

Scene. Rather than let his mentally ill sister be taken by a social worker, Arthur has tried to enroll the social worker, Jeff, in their games. He has failed, and the sister is leaving with Jeff.

ARTHUR:

You could have been extraordinary, Jeff. You've got a start, you're a fast learner. But are you a man who can transform the world? Before you take my sister, you be sure. Because that's what it takes. You can't just lead her out into space and leave her there. A ward, a shelter, pawn her off on someone else, visit on weekends. You'll lose her. Right down the black hole. Be sure. That's my life you're taking. You have be vigilant, 24/7. And not just the hours, you go where she wants. Travel with her, you go in her worlds. Down deep. And give the rest up. Don't try to hold on, that's my advice. The hour of the day, the time, the light, you'll find that it's porous. Roll with the perception. That's how it's done. Don't try to hold on. That was my mistake. Can't do both worlds, hers and yours, that's where I went wrong. End up in the beanie bin. Now *that's* a problem. Hole gets twice as deep. You try to get a grip, they zap your wires. Vzzzzt! Climb outta that, they hit you with the needle. Deep, that's deep.

(Staring, lost in it, unraveling…)

Don't..hold..on. You have to surrender. Let goooooo… Roooll, rolling, down deep where the serpents roll. Mammoth great white things rolling. And you won't know, if you made it up, or that's your mind now, rolling…. You manifest…until…you roll… it. Turn it over, up & down, inside out, white to black, and stretch it out… Black sheet plastered to the sky! … Poke it full of pins for stars … And take it home, to Annie!

(HE laughs)

They had no idea, Mama, the psychs, what they did for us, ruining my brain! All the more for us, right Annie? Planets! Stars! Light up the sky! You have no idea what it is to create *the world!* And you have no world 'till you see it reflected in her eyes! You have no world…

(His smile drains away.)

No world. There is… no world..

"78 Horses"

From *Fiona's Mane*

Scene: Emotionally fragile and obsessive-compulsive, Fiona explains to a new friend what she has that makes life worth living.

FIONA:

I have horses. 78 of them at present. Not live ones of course, but porcelain, pottery, china, marble, and some plastic, but very good plastic, well made. Mares and stallions, no geldings. I think it's wrong to geld a horse. It breaks their spirit. They're never the same. It steals the life force. Somebody gave me a gelding once. I put it out the window. It's still there, on the ledge. It's better this way. He couldn't make it with the others. They're all stronger than him. Plus he's damaged. his mane is chipped. And you can't tell me it doesn't matter. It's my herd. I know how it is. That's just life. You can put that horse among others, but that won't make it fit in. There's a space between him and the others all the time, whether I put him in the middle of the crowd, dead center, or whether he wakes up one morning and finds them all gone. All you can do is stand...on your own legs.. and try to feel the strength in them... and the earth below you, if it has any power to give you... And try to graze on good clean food you were meant to eat -- not just taste it as you chew, but also hear the grass tearing as you go... And try to stand with your head up, so you can feel a little bit of wind in your mane. That's a good thing. Those are things just as important as anything. Whether you're in the herd or not.

"Helping Me With a Painting"

From *Three To Get Ready*

Scene: Moira and Lo are mutually unsocial neighbors, which is why asking a favor is nearly intolerable for Moira…

MOIRA:

Um, before I go… I need to ask… Well, y'see, Lanie was helping me with a painting. The other day, you know when, well. It's just, um, how do I put it… I'd like to finish it. The painting. It's… well, it's got me kind of stuck. See, Lanie was making suggestions. And I followed them. So I'd just, y'know, like to get his input, to finish. His help. Be brief, won't take long.

(Sees she is unconvincing.)

I understand, what it was you said, about not having people in. I don't myself. I mean *really* I don't. But he, well, got in the apartment, and it was very, I found myself painting to entertain him, y'know, keep him from touching things, and, he just made these suggestions. To the painting – And I don't even do that, I don't take suggestions in my work, but, as you know, he's just real persistent – And that's okay, you want to stay open to the unexpected, even when it's hard to tolerate, because life is an, a banquet really, of possibilities, so I wanted to do that. But, it was really more of his format, y'know?

(Still getting no response, Moira is starting to grow unhinged.)

I just really need to finish it, and I, a person can't just *intuit* somebody else's format, can they? So… It would be very nice if he could just – I don't leave things unfinished! Okay? I don't do well with that, it makes it difficult to rest, so I just need him for a couple of minutes. Really. Nothing's going to happen, I don't do this, okay?! I don't ask! I don't bother people! I completely agree with you, you shouldn't go into people's homes. But he got in, and started this thing, and I just really need to be able to get some sleep!

"Makin' Worlds"

From *Midsummer Madness*

Scene: *Fat Larry, the lighting guy, introduces his new assistant to the equipment room of an   old community theater.*

FAT LARRY:

Ah, the glamour a the theatre.

(Comes in, starts rummaging in equipment.)

You know lights? Of course not, why would they gimmie a lighting assistant who knows lights? You know beer? If you know beer, I can teach ya the rest. Ya gotcher leko's, yer fresnels, yer barn doors...

(Slides metal plate out of one.)

Yer lost gobo. THANKS FOR PUTTING EVERYTHING IN ITS PLACE! This is a gobo.

(Throws it in a box.)

Anyway, you'll catch on. The important thing is, get fat. That's how ya tell the techies from the talent. Now, the main thing ya gotta know about workin' in the theater? Theater people are all fuckin' crazy. But not crazy in a bad way, y'know? It's like, they wanna create somethin', that doesn't exist yet, and what that is, is a whole world! Ya know? I mean like worlds with people, and light, and *meaning*. Right? Profound. And car mechanics, they can't say that. They can't wake up in the morning & go, "Fuck, I got a world to make today!" And that's theater. I love it, man. I do. It *is* magic. And I'm fat? Which is why they call me Fat Larry? But we make the light, man. So never think your job isn't important. Every person in theater counts. And some people go, 'Oh, well, I'm just gettin' the lint off the costumes," but every little thing is an element that makes that world. And one thing for sure? Without lighting, that world would be fuckin' dark!

"Too Many to Count"

From *Fiona's Mane*

Scene: Fiona, who has obsessive compulsive disorder, has gotten into a conversation with a man who is in recovery. As they find what they have in common, she opens up about her disorder.

FIONA:

61 days. You have 61 days. And I have two and a half years. Since...

(Makes a smoking gesture.)

Yes. I still count. You're not supposed to, when you quit, but I do anyway. Count. Everything. Days. Hours. Trains. Oranges. It's... I can't not. People, steps, hats, clocks, dogs, pencils, pens, forks... Soothing, it's soothing. But exhausting. You have five buttons on your shirt, 12 shoes lace holes, three zippers, two on your sweatshirts and one on your pan – And five cats, you have five cats, and a geranium on every table, I don't know how many tables.

I have six tablecloths. No plants. I don't keep plants. Too many germs. Or cats. Very bad, with cats, very unclean. Lick themselves, and then one another, very unsanitary! That's – no, it's very bad to have that, very dangerous. There's just so much the immune system can stand and then it's, you break down. From the *germs*! They crawl. And there's just so many! Oh! Too many to count! There's too many to count, you, you can't count them, and it's very bad! I have to get home! I have to – Ew, I can't – the filth, I have to get home, there's too many to count!

"A Short Thread"

From *The Last Nickel*

Scene: Watching her sister Jo reenact her own death, Jamie can only bring the scene to a halt by admitting why she has insomnia.

JAMIE:

I cut your respirator, okay?! It was me! And you'd have done the same if you'd seen yourself, with your face all bloated and your brain coming out the back of your head. Which didn't even happen 'til they tried to lift the car off you and dropped it. My sister Jo, irreversibly, irrevocably brain dead. When they said you were in a vegetative state, I just wanted you to sit up and say, "A vegetable? What kind, Pennsylvania parsnips?" P-word. Plosives are funny, right?

There's wasn't a doubt in me, the last thing you'd want was to lie there with empty eyes and have mom & dad watch you shrivel up. Jesus! It was scary, but it wasn't that hard. All I had to do was picture you pinned under the car, and cut it. And you know what? You'll like this, Jo, you know what I cut it with? Uncle Jack's old hunting knife. That he gave you 'cause you couldn't go to school that day? It was really only a short thread. When that was the only thing holding you from freedom, it didn't seem like much to cut. I thought it would cut you loose. I just didn't know it was the only thing holding me to the world.

"When I Go"

From *Cold Shadow*

Scene: Last speech of the condemned.

MARSE:

Today is the first day of the rest of your life. That's a saying. 'Course, nobody ever really said it. It's just one'a those things on posters.

Well, today *is* the first day of the rest of my life. You may think that's pretty weird, considering in a little bit they're gonna gimmie the drip. But hey, nobody ever said how long the rest of your life would be. I mean whadda you think, life's forever? Yeah, I know what you think. You're thinkin' about tomorrow. You got plans for tomorrow, tomorrow's calendar is full, you think you got a tomorrow. Well, ladies and gentlemen, I'm here to tell you, there's no guarantee. Once you got a moment in your hands, it's now. And in end, that's all ya got. Look at me. I'm flesh and blood, tomorrow I'll be gone. This is the first day of the rest of my life and it ain't just a saying anymore. And I wish I knew then what I know now. Life wouldn'a seemed so cheap. If I could leave you anything, I'd give you that. When you watch me die, you sit back there and you'l know, this here is the only day of your life.

"Life Becomes Art"

From *Eating the Dead*

Scene: Brea, (pronounced "Bray-uh"), a painter, grows expansive in the face of her lover Shay's return.

BREA:

If you knew how difficult it was, you would understand. Now that Shay is back, I have the balance! You have to have all the right elements to do your best work. Because it's not simple, to do one's art. It's physical, it's emotional, it makes demands on your spirit, it's mathematical! And when you achieve that, the technical knowledge, the passion, the opportunity, then míja, then, you are just coming to the hard part. Because to get from here to there...

(Points from her heart to the painting.)

...you are going to have to admit that you still don't have it all. And never will. And you must take that despair, and all your blindness and pain, and use that. We are fundamentally imperfect. We're made that way, like the Indian art where they leave an imperfection so the spirit can get in. I am incomplete. And if you will admit that, and be willing to use it, the emptiness will show you the way. It leads your hand. And the work becomes part of your healing. And you aren't ready to make art, or do anything real, until you realize that you don't come to the art to complete it, you come to it to help complete you. That's why it means so much, to have her back. To help me face my incompleteness. To use it. Because when you can do that, life becomes art.

PHOTO
GALLERY

Select photographs from

original New York productions

Russell Jones as Shaquay in Circle East's
production of **Fiona's Mane** *(photo Michele Coleman)*

Donna Jean Fogel as 2 in the Circle Rep
Lab's production of **Nine** *(photo Susan Michie)*

Lou Sumrall as Hershal and Suzan Postel as the Angel
In The LAB Theatre Company's **Prelude to Walking**

*Katherine Brealt-Gooch as Hostetta in Vital Theatre
Company's* **Ducks Crossing** *(photo Sun Productions Inc.)*

Gregor Paslawsky in Wings Theater's
A Rage of Chaos *(photo Jane Shepard)*

Kate Bennis as Jamie & George Sheffey operating Tim The Pig in
The Last Nickel *at One Dream Theatre (photo Julie Hamberg)*

George Sheffey as Arthur and Tom Johnson as Jeff in The Barrow Group's **Glass Jaw** *(photo Travis McHale)*

Vanessa Shealy as Lanie in Vital Theatre's **Friends of the Deceased** *(photo Sun Productions Inc.)*

Nell Mooney and Jane Shepard in Circle East's **Reap the Wild Historian** *(photo Susan Michie)*

Jon Krupp as Bob Bean in Vital Theatre's
Ducks Crossing *(photo Julie Hamberg)*

Kenneth Simmons as Fletch in
HellEden *at Wings Theatre*

Danielle Delgado as Brea in
Live Theatre's **Eating the Dead**
(photo Chris Jones)

Pamela Dunlap as Vi
In Vital Theatre's
Friends of the Deceased

Johnny Sanchez as Reynaldo in Live Theatre's **Eating the Dead** *(photo Chris Jones)*

Jane Shepard as The Lecturer in Vital Theater's **Idiot's Guide to the Brain** *(photo Shawn Hirabayashi)*

Kit Flanagan as Kelli in **Commencing** *at HERE*

SHORT

ONE-PERSON PLAYS

The Good Drum

God Is A Dyke

Long Distance

A Rage of Chaos

The Good Drum

CAST:
One man, in prison jumpsuit and handcuffs

SETTING:
No set required.
An empty stage is preferable

*(**At rise:** A man in an orange jumpsuit walks onstage: EDDIE. HIS wrists are handcuffed in the front, and HE fiddles with an unlit cigarette. From time to time HE casts nervous glances at unseen figures offstage. HE addresses audience.)*

EDDIE:

I would like to apologize first of all, to Mr. Lispenard and to the people who have tried to help me. Mr. Lispenard has been a very nice man, and has brought me comic books and also cigarettes and stuff during my incarceration, and tried really hard and didn't treat me like I was bad. He treated me like a good person and always dressed up nice for the courts and smelled good and all, and if any of you is ever in trouble I would like to recommend you to speak to Warner Lispenard.

Also I would like to thank my mother who is in heaven, because she too believed I was a good person, and that is hard when a boy grows as big as me and is confused in their ways, and I wish she was here, although not today.

And I also want to thank my sister Cathy, even though she did not come to see me or what happened at court because she is a good Christian. And I just like her.

Second of all, I would like to say, that I did not regret the killing because it was the money I wanted and it is easy to pull the trigger and not that hard to shoot someone.

It doesn't take you any effort at all, and you would be surprised if you did it. You just shoot and they're dead and then I had the money. So. I regret that now though, since of how it turned out. I would like people to know I am sorry because they said in the trial how they suffered. I am sure the people I killed were very nice and I'm sorry they're dead, although I can not really picture how that would be on their end.

Then last of all, I don't have anything much, but there are these comics that I had in jail, that Mr. Lispenard is holding. I am leaving them in my will to Kenny Alter. I am not sure that he will want them. They are almost all Batman. I think they are good, especially the art. But Mr. Alter may not take them, in light of my killing his wife. I killed her with gun and my hands, but comic books is all I have.

Mr. Alter is who pushed for this situation, so I guess it will be better after I am dead too.

(HE puts a unlit cigarette in his mouth.)

EDDIE:

I don't get a light for this, but I am going to hold it in my mouth because it is a comfort to me. I don't have any family here, so I am a bit nervous. I don't know if God counts as family or not.

But, okay, so I would like to have Mr. Alter to have my comic books, and that's all. If he would take them. Because he has had a bad shock. I don't feel sorry for him because I am a sociopath and they tell me I don't know how it feels for other people.

And I don't.

But I think maybe the media is a sociopath too, because they don't seem to know how other people feel either. Because they print all those things and had that show on showing her body, and that must have made Mr. Alter feel bad, I don't know, but they also put that stuff in about how I am a sociopath and that I am the "Point Blank Murderer."

I don't think in terms of point blank. I think in terms of comic books.

What did the cow say to the ducks? "Wanna have milk & quackers"? I know, it's bad, but Skinny told me on the row in the middle of the night and it really cracked me up. And also, I am nervous.

In Olaire there was only one drugstore and Batman was the only comic book they carried. So I became fond of it. And I got them also at the K.P. in the service. Batman is afraid of nothing and only demented because he saw his parents get shot. And that made his mind a little off. But he goes after only bad guys.

I did not expect to become one of the bad guys. When I read comic books, I always thought in terms of being like the hero, and saving people. There wasn't a lot of people to save in Olaire. I didn't really save *anybody* in Olaire. I didn't find anybody to save. Except Sharon, and it was hard to save her because, y'know, she didn't really see me as a hero. I thought I did some pretty good boyfriend things, but it wasn't like performing feats. There just weren't any feats, any heroic feats to be done. And in the army we didn't do anything. So I didn't feel either like a bad guy or a good guy.

But I always thought more like Batman So I don't know how it ended up this way. I was good to dogs, and did good duty, and wrote my mom when she was alive. But I couldn't find anybody, not really anybody, to be heroic to. And then after Sharon left there wasn't anybody at all. But it's not like my heart wasn't on the job!

EDDIE:

If anybody here needed a good job done I would be a good person to ask! I have a heart beating inside me, just like you. And I'm not saying don't kill me, but I'm like the drum, the good Indian drum in Eagle Scouts? Somebody keeps the rhythm and everybody else does something to it, like a war cry or oath, but one person keeps the beat and that's the beating of goodness, and my heart's like that. And once I pulled a dog out of the mud.

(HE looks off to the side nervously.)

I have to go in a minute.

(Remembering on fingers)

So, there was Batman, and Warren... and Cathy, and um... Mr. Alter. And the good drum. And God. People said I am not going to God because of my sins, but I am because God forgives everything and Skinny said if I have any doubts to listen to my own heart, because that's the sound of the good drum. You can hear your heart if you put your ear against your pillow. Try it tonight. That's the sound of the good drum.

(Looks off again, feeling hurried.)

Um, I have one more thing to say.

I guess I don't sound all that sharp, because I am on valium. But it's not valium, I never did sound all that sharp. People tell me that, it never did bother me. So what, I'm not sharp, you're not batman either, so fuck you.

Sorry. I wish I could have a smoke because I am quite addicted to nicotine. But, whatever, they gave me a carton, I had plenty, I am just nervous.

I really have to go.

I wanted to say thanks to the lady who wrote me the cards, but I don't re-member her name. The card with the flowers.

(He turns to go, hesitates, turns back.)

I want Mr. Alter to take my comic books! I just wish he would. I am afraid they will go to waste and, and Batman had a good drum, he had a good drum, he was demented but his feats are good. And maybe they will give Mr. Alter some guidance!

(HE looks out at back of audience to Kenny Alter.)

EDDIE:

Mr. Alter, I wish you would take some guidance! I am going to get shots in a little while and then I won't trouble you anymore, but your face on the TV. is like that dog in the mud! It's, it's all screwed up and shaky, sir! It's stuck in trouble, and God will forgive me, but you will be down here still and I think, if you would just read them, nevermind that they're from me, you will see that a demented heart can still do good! And you will have to get out of the mud! I can not do anything more for you! --

(EDDIE pulls open the top of his jumpsuit, showing his heart)

But I wish I could give you this! I wish you could take it! This is the real thing I have. I'm afraid it will be wasted.

(HE turns to go again.)

When you go home tonight, turn your ear to the pillow, and listen. That will be the Good Drum.

(HE lifts his head, and walks off the stage.)

God Is A Dyke

CAST:

One Brooklyn dyke, big boots, leather jacket

SETTING:

No set is required
beyond a metal garbage can

(Bare stage. STAGE LIGHTS are still at pre-set and HOUSE LIGHTS still on when JESSIE walks out on stage. SHE is a young woman in a leather jacket, fingerless gloves, bandana, and big boots. Very Brooklyn. SHE calls to booth.)

JESSIE:

Yeah, okay. Let's get on with it.

> *(House LIGHTS go out, STAGE LIGHTS UP. SHE looks a bit like a dear caught in the head- lights. Acknowledges audience nervously.)*

Whoa. I dunnow if you ever done this, stood up on a stage like this, but it's very, very weird. Can't see shit.

> *(Signifies stage wings)*

An' that..space..very weird, what is that? I feel like little elves are gonna come out or somethin'... *(Munchkins)* "Come out, come out, wherever you are..." Well, I came out. No pun intended. "An' now a very nice dyke will come out an' discuss her philosophy."

Yeah, right. I'm afraid I got very little to share on the subject. What I know, you prob'ly already heard. An if you *don't* know it, you prob'ly didn't care to learn it. An' if you don't know it & you *do* care, ya prob'ly wouldn't understand it, & even if ya *do* an' ya *do*, who the fuck knows what you're talkin' about anyhow?! So! Putz with the philosophy. "Never poke a stick up a dog's ass." There's with your philosophy. Or, no, wait a minnit...!

> *(JESSIE drags an old metal GARBAGE CAN from the side of the stage, emptying out the trash carelessly.)*

Oo, they shoulda never turned me loose...

> *(SHE pulls a jumbo marker out of her jacket and writes on the bottom of the can. Shows it to audience...)*

There! Da Da! "SHIT HAPPENS." Does that span the philosophical map or what? Whatever ya believe, this covers it. "Hey, babe, you lost your wallet? I got a spare hundred, take it, shit happens." "Yo, weege, your friend never paid me back, hadda take his thumbs, y'know, shit happens."

> *(SHE smiles at audience, on a roll now...)*

JESSIE:

Such philosophy, I think, is why the bible is so big. Plays it both ways. 'Turn the other cheek' & 'Eye for an eye' under the same cover. Very handy! Whichever way ya wanna play it. Now my sister-in-law, she's Catholic, no wonder she's schizophrenic, right? God: the judgmental father, Jesus: a compulsively forgiving son, very conflicted family! An' Mary: whoa there's a case: "I got pregnant without nookie. You believe that, I'll forgive anything!"

(JESSIE stops herself, self-conscious again.)

Whoa. I digress. Royally. I should chill. Do some meditation. An' I know this chick, right, she meditates? Most cool Buddhist babe, very righteous, in body as well as mind -- a body I would not kick outta my bed, let me not lie, even if I do digress, the woman makes me want to moan, faint an' *die!* An' her philosophy, very close to "Shit Happens". So, no wonder she got peace, what's to argue? Don't chant so loud? Don't meditate so close to the shrubbery?

'Course, I never seen a Buddhist on the battle field. "Joe, Joe, we're goin' on patrol! You wanna come?" "Yeah, gimmie a minute to meditate." "Joe, Joe, they blew your leg off! You wanna meditate?" "Fuck no, kill all those motherfuckers!"

Yeah, it's when the goin' gets rough, you find out what you really believe, right? That's when it counts. All of a sudden, how you look at it becomes very important. Like say, just for the sake of example...

(Gets GARBAGE CAN.)

This is you.

(SHE touches its shape.)

Got your own individuations, a nick here or there, but basically, very smooth.

(Lays can on its side.)

You roll into life...

(JESSIE rolls the can.)

Very nice. There you are. Now, I, for this sophisticated demonstration, will represent ...

(Goes backstage, comes out with HAMMER.)

JESSIE:

...Life!

(Goes to can.)

Certain things, occurrences of life, are gonna shape you...

(SHE looks at the garbage can with intent.)

Say, bus accident...

(Raises hammer.)

No. Not a accident.

(SHE puts the hammer down.)

More like, human nature. The look. The touch. The silence in a room. That does this to you...

(With a sudden violent vehemence, SHE stomps the can a good one with her boot, leaving the barrel dented and misshapen.)

Okay. Now we have effect. Somethin' has occurred. An' from now on...

(JESSIE pushes the garbage can, it rolls unevenly.)

You will never move through life the same. That's the shape a you now. You ain't never gonna go back. So. Now you gotta decide. How you gonna look at it? Are you permanently damaged? Or will you merely roll differently? This, I think, is the real question. You want a philosophy? You answer that. Very tricky.

(SHE pulls herself away, trying to avoid anything too heartfelt.)

Myself, I don't care. I got no answers. Whatever gets ya through the night, as Janis Joplin said. Get it while ya can.

(Noting CAN.)

Can. Get it? Yeah, garbage humor.

JESSIE: *(To GARBAGE CAN.)*

I found it funny, didn't you?

Well, this is nice. I'm standin' here talkin' to garbage. "How was your theatrical evening?" "Oh very nice, Jewish dyke talkin' to a trash can."

(Looks at CAN.)

Well, little can. Whadda ya got to say?

(Waits for reply.)

Silence. Never gonna get over it if you don't talk about it. You don't wanna talk to me, talk to God.

'Course, there's no guarantee he's listenin'. Prob'ly watchin' the ball game. Otherwise how come he lets all this terrible stuff happen, right? Or, as my old man used to say, "If God is listenin' he just heard me say go fuck yourself!" There's philosophy. Nice guy.

Hard to believe he come from his mother. Now my Gramma, *she* got philosophy! "Bubby, kids at school think I'm weird!" "Eh, that's life." "Bubby, dad kicked me outta the house!" "Eh, that's life." "Bubby, you know that girl I was stayin' with? I can't stay there no more 'cause her mom caught us havin' oral sex!" "Eh..."

(BUBBY hesitates, then shrugs it off.)

"What the hell, it's all life!"

Some people got God, some got destiny, or philosophy, or botany, though I dunnow what that is, bugs or somethin', and *some* people got the philosophy a pokin' holes in other people's philosophy. "Sure, Jessie, you look for God! But don't expect to find him if you comin' to church dressed like that! You wanna live that 'lifestyle', Jesus ain't savin' you."

Well fine. Maybe God is some big old straight guy sittin' up there. But maybe he ain't. Maybe God's a little old lady in Brooklyn, heard the term 'oral sex' for the first time in her 85 years, said, "That's life!"

Or maybe God is me in a leather jacket! Ain't nothin' makes me feel more heavenly than this! -- An' by the way, lemme tell ya, if God is a dyke, ain't one'a you gettin' into heaven without much, much better boots! Boots & a jacket, yeah, totally divine. Eight years I been wearin' this one, since when I come out as a lesbian. Yeah, that's right, you gotta say the word. Lesbian!

JESSIE:

Big Dyke. God or no God. Sin or no sin. Life or death. You are what you are. And if you ain't, you got no life anyway.

You get lucky enough to meet somebody makes your heart sing, I don't care *who* it is, you better walk that walk. An' lemme tall ya, baby, we did! Walk it, dance it, me & Sharon, we done every dyke march since we been together! Day before the pride parade. Demonstrated our asses off in Washington! We're marchin' along, & Sharon all of sudden drops trou on the street & moons her ass right at the White House! Damn!

They didn't even notice. I noticed. Go to all the parties, gay & lesbian center, very excellent dancer,

oo, I just stand by like, "Is she incredible? She mine!" Fourth anniversary, got the tattoos. Domestic partnership last year, city a New York, wearin' yours truly, thank you very much. Last summer, we was sittin' in the diner, 7th avenue, Park Slope, man comes in, stops at our table, & says, "Know how I knew you was lezzies? The leather jackets." An' he lifts up his arm, an' he's got a baseball bat.

An' I see Sharon's eyes get real big, and I start to stand up, an' I heard this 'thunk.' An' suddenly I'm lyin' on the wet linoleum, an' I got a helluva headache, an' I'm thinkin', "Somethin' about this is not right." An' I hear this sound. There's this *absolute silence* in the room. An' in it, I hear this 'thunk'! 'Thunk!' 'Thunk!' An' it sounds to me like somebody puttin' dents in a garbage can. An' I just can't figure out why I'm lyin' on the floor and somebody's poundin' dents in a garbage can.

An' then I see this blood on the linoleum, runnin' towards me. An' I'm thinkin', "It's such a shame. I can't move, & it's gonna stain the jacket."

Life becomes very, very lonely, in that moment. You don't feel like no big tough dyke. You feel like just some little six year old, stained your dress, an' now you can't get outta the way. There is no philosophy for this time. You are alone. You can't make that sound stop. An' you ain't never gonna go back. No matter what you do. You only get to go on. Very tricky. One of these very tricky times, findin' a way to go on. I mean, you do go on. But to... go forward... in life...

> *(SHE struggles a moment, wanting to lighten up,*
> *back off the subject, but too late. Looks around,*
> *stranded onstage. Tries to joke.)*

JESSIE:

I mean, I don't even wanna go forward from here. I, I, I could leave this stage right now actually. an' you'd all be sittin' there goin', "What the fuck was that?! What the hell kind of a story is that?!" Oughtta stick to talkin' to cans, huh?

They ain't never caught him though. They was all so stunned, they said. He just walked right out. In the silence. Walkin' around now.

One can see where a specific philosophy would come of assistance. 'Cause everybody gonna have a time, see, like this, when all them things what make the world make sense don't mean jack shit. All in a flash, no more. Thunk. What'dya got then, y'know? "Shit happens"?

I got 52 stitches. Got a scar that people envy when they're comparin' scars. The hearin' loss they don't envy, left hand still not hot, and I got a voice runnin' in my head, oh yeah, I got a voice talkin' to me all the time tellin' me this man should *not be free.*

An' it is not wise to walk around, come in public with these things in your head, better you should go to synagogue an' pray, but this is tricky also, because every minute you find yourself prayin', "God, lemme find the guy, lemme just once meet this fuck on a dark street, this man, who could beat a woman to death with a bat!"

Not a dyke in a leather jacket, who's lying right there in front of you, but a school teacher, just turned 34, who was reachin' down to me, that's all, just reachin' out with her gentle hands, and he…

She don't even wear the jacket except on weekends, she don't take it to school 'cause kids need somebody they look up to and who respects 'em & looks nice for 'em, because they count, & who wears.. who wears a little bit a perfume, jaw line an' wrist, very delicate wrist, so they see how a little bit a scent, just for yourself, shows self respect. Won't even go to brunch before 12:30 on Sunday 'cause she gotta go to church & talk with God. "Bye, Jessie, see ya in a bit, gotta go talk with God now!" And if God is listenin' right now he's hearin' me say Go fuck yourself!

'Cause nobody deserves to be believed in who lets that happen. She was the kind of person we needed on this earth! Not me, I wouldn'a mind I died, I was right there an' it should'a been me, I got nothin' more to offer this world anyhow. I got no more songs in my heart, sorry, Sharon, but it's true. This can is completely flat!

(SHE stomps the can.)

JESSIE:

I wish to God you was here, honey, cause you would'a known what to do. You would still be standin', you'da rose above it an' said, "I will not be stopped." Her hands would be reachin' out still, goin', "Don't worry honey, I'm here, & I am gonna lift you up!"

(SHE lifts the can above her head.)

"I will lift you up and show you to a world where people murder with a bat!" An' you would say, "By the power of love in me, you fuckin' sons of bitches, if you wanna stop me, it will take more than *dents*!

(JESSIE slams the can down.)

An' if God don't stand for that, then God *will* be a dyke in a leather jacket! A great big, fat lesbian in the sky who will raise us above this *mess*!" And you would say, like you did a long time ago when I told you I couldn't make love, "It's up to you. Are you permanently damaged, or will you merely roll differently?"

(SHE gathers herself a moment. No more effort to avoid anything. Simple & alone.)

Well I'm not God. An' Sharon ain't here. An' I would give anything, anything her blue eyes was still lookin' on this world. But it's just me. An' I will not be stopped. If we truly don't got no say about what happens... If all we get is how you look at it... then somehow, some way... we all gonna need much, much better boots.

(SHE stands a moment, looking out, relieved.)

Well, I gotta get off this stage now.

(Looks at smashed can, glances offstage.)

Somebody's gonna be really pissed. You see somebody later, they ask you what the fuck happened to their trash can, you just look 'em in the eye & say, "So what? Now it rolls different."

(JESSIE smiles, turns, and walks off the stage, leaving the can where it is.)

Long Distance

CAST:

Roy Gannoy

SETTING:

Roy's living room.

A seedy armchair and side table can suffice.

(ROY enters his apartment, talking to audience, high energy. As HE speaks, HE proceeds to put down his things, take off his coat, and don a seedy bathrobe.)

ROY:

Do you know what happened today? Oh! I couldn't wait to tell you! You will die! Do you know who I saw? Fatima Farterweigh! From the third grade, the one in the class picture caught for all eternity touching her tongue to her nose?! -- Oh! I cannot get over that! Not for a thousand years and all the yen in yigamoo! Can you imagine the humiliation?! I combed my hair at least 12 times for that picture, not a pasty hair out of place! I lived in terror a tweak would have fallen down, and momma would point and Alvin would scoff at me and I would live a condemned life!

But Fatima! Fat Fatima! Oh, not fat, I shouldn't say fat, that's mean, um... Pudgy -- no, not pudgy -- plump! Generous. No! Rubenesque. Okay, that's not it but let's pretend it is so we can get on with it, okay? Okay! *Rubenesque* Fatima Farterweigh, imbedded into that picture with brillo hair and her tongue up her nose... One eye going this way and one eye going that! Oh! It frightens me, it chills me, *burned* into my memory!

So! I am walking across the plaza, and this, this petrified photographic image is transformed before memory's eye into a living, breathing, grown-up Fatima Farterweigh! Standing before me, frowning, just like she was in third grade, all pimply – Ew, do third graders even have pimples?! -- And do you know what she did? She pointed at me and shouted, *"You!"* And I tried to pretend that I hadn't seen her, but it didn't work very well because I was so surprised I was just staring, and she shouted, *"Roy!"* And, I have to tell you, I said, *"Me? No!"* And she absolutely screamed, *"Roy Gannoy!"* And -- what could I do? She chased me across the plaza screaming, *"Roy Gannoy the Bubble Boy!"* I shouted back, *"I don't know you, and for God's sake, Fatima, stop screaming!"* Oh! Can you believe it? I am so lame! But I was absolutely cornered!

And Fatima Farterweigh goes, *"You're Roy Gannoy, that boy who talked to himself and blew bubbles all alone on the playground!"* Well. I just turned to her and said, *"And you're Fat Fatima who's going to fart-her-way to fourth grade!"*

And she stopped, and said, *"But that was mean."*

And I said, *"So were all of you!"* Yes I did. I said that. That put a crimp in her bonnet. She says, *"I remember you now, you were always mean."*

And I said, *"No, I was witty."*

ROY:

This is a common misconception. If you're a man you can be witty, but if you have ironic insight as an eight-year-old, you're mean. -- Although, apparently, if you blow bubbles or talk to yourself at any age, no one will ever, *ever* forget it!

And do you know what Fatima said then?

She smiles and goes, *"Do you still talk to what's-his-name?"*

"No, Fatima, I don't see anyone from third grade, I don't know what you're talking about."

"No, not a student! That thing you did, your little playground friend!"

I said, *"I don't talk to anyone."*

"No, your special friend."

I did not know what to say. I do not know what to say to people like that, to this day, I don't, period, goodnight. She leers and says, *"The one you always talked to on the playground. You're the one who had an invisible friend."*

Okay, fat girl, the cat is out of the bag! Do you still pick your pimples?! Do you still eat your boogers?! Are you still inflated with enough hot air to blow yourself to fourth grade?! Yes, apparently you still are! Well, of course I didn't say that. I didn't say, "Fat Fatima Fart-her-way to fourth grade hair like a brillo pad sucking snot out of her sinuses in the school picture, eyes doing this: ga ga ga!" No! I didn't say that!

And then she, she who has to shop for clothes at the *Hindenburg* factory, says, *"I was mean too. I just didn't know how to tell anybody I liked them. Did you?"*

Fatima Farterweigh... I shrugged. I said, *"I never liked anybody."*

She says, *"Oh, that's sad."*

Can you imagine? I said, *"No. It's not. It's witty."*

And she said, *"No, Roy, that's sadder than me."*

I said, *"But, you're Fat Fatima Fart-her-way to the fourth grade, wall-eyed & licked your nose in the picture and everybody hated you, even me."*

"I know," she said, *"But I liked you."*

> *(Silence for a bit, as HE noogles around, not sure how to respond.)*

Well... I could have told her I guess. I could have told her about you. I could have said, Fatima, girl who turned out to actually like me... I don't *need* to be liked. Because I no longer have that invisible friend that I talked to. Now I go home and put on my robe and talk to an entire *room* full of them!

I have *masses* at my disposal whenever I need them! -- I've made up more people than you will ever know in your life, I've talked to more different kinds of people -- Oh, I talk with friends, family, me & momma gab up a storm! She loves gossip now the way she never did when she was alive! Sometimes I sit Alvin down right here and read him the riot act about the way he treated me & momma and, let me tell you, in *this* house, *this* time around, he's sorry! And how he & momma should have had a little brother for me, even a sickly one, I would have watched out for him. And I talk with my little brother.

Hm-mm! It's not everyone who gets to decide whether or not they have a baby brother. Sure, he can be a pest -- when he's in his teens, he's unbearable! Doesn't listen to a thing I say. I tell him. But he's a good boy basically. And when he's not, I make him a neurosurgeon! Yes! And I am so not a jealous big brother. I'm the kind that attends his medical graduation and gives the talk!

> *(Behind chair, as podium, giving speech.)*

"No brother could be more proud than I, to look upon the young man sitting here today, and know that that little hand, that I taught to tie shoes, will be used in the service of mankind. Congratulations, Gary." Gary, after Gary Cooper.

When Gary's not around I hold sálons! Oh yes, right here in my room! In my robe! People love to gather here, excellent meals, but always casual.

Henry Kissinger, Truman Capote, Dorothy Parker, Britney Spears -- don't laugh, Britney is very much underrated. And cute as a button! I admit, Truman & Dorothy make merciless fun when she's out of the room. I smooth things over.

> *(Looking out over all the audience.)*

Debutantes, dilettantes, dignitaries. Common hairdressers, businessmen, poets, those with hard traveling. All of you! You are mine! I adore you. So!

ROY:

There is no lack of a listening ear in this room! Is there? I could have told her all of that.

And for a moment, for a fleeting moment, it passed through my mind to do it. To tell her everything! Just... let it all rip, even bring her home, introduce her around! It was funny, I must say, the urge, the funniest sort of... bubble. I suppose I might have told her that I had sort of liked her too.

All I said was, *"I have to go now."*

To her, you understand, I will always be Roy Gannoy the Bubble Boy. The kid who talks to himself and has no friends. A product of their limited minds.

So! Fatima, in her coat -- she had this horrendous, oh-dear-God-what-did-you-hit-with-the-truck, dead fur thing on! Yes. And this, this slightly crooked front tooth when she smiled. And pudgy hands. Very soft. Pudgy, quite soft hands, that shook yours firmly, not mean, just firm. And she said, *"Well, I have to go back to the stand anyhow, we're selling long distance cards, because it's a better deal than Sprint, you don't need a long distance card do you?"* And I told her I didn't.

She said, *"Goodbye, Roy."* And she walked away across the plaza. A waddling wave of green & yellow muumuu. Soft green. And soft yellow. Back to her long distance cards.

So! That was my day! I absolutely had to tell you before I popped! Oh! What a weird, weird venture! *Never* touch your tongue to your nose when a camera is anywhere in the vicinity, that's all. You will never escape it. I am so glad to be home. With you. All comfy.

I still... I feel... the funniest kind of twinge still. Curiosity I think. Which is natural. Ironic, really, for me. In passing. I just... I wonder, in retrospect is all, what exactly the cost of long distance is these days.

(*HE sits staring vaguely into space.*

LIGHTS FADE.)

A Rage of Chaos

CAST:

A man in a white suit

SETTING:

The dining room of a country bed & breakfast

Requires chair, table, props

SETTING: The dining room of a country bed & breakfast. A MAN enters, wearing a white suit, addresses audience.)

MAN:

Brw, boo, whoo! Nippy, isn't it? Oh, mm, achem.

(Coughs, sniffs, gets out HANDKERCHIEF, wipes nose, blows, hacks up.)

Oh, mm, 'scuse me! Absolutely appalling. I *beg* your pardon. Wow! It's nippy.

(Goes to window, looking out.)

Look at all that green. I once told someone I thought all the green was a bit tedious. God must be a bit demented on green. Overdone! But maybe that's because I'm a city person, grass always looks to me like something undeveloped: "What is this? Did somebody forget to build something here? Please. Scenery! Green control, please!"

(Paint gesture.)

Whob, whob. Small man-made garden, trees planted judiciously, flowers here & there, *patches* of grass, very nice. Uncontrolled? Very frightening. Foliage overkill. "No placement" as Te-- as some people might say. Just a rage of chaos.

(Uses hanky again.)

God does rage.

That's a good one though, isn't it? A "rage of chaos"? A gaggle of geese, a coven of crows, a pride of lions, bevy of quail, set of badgers, pod of dolphins, skulk of foxes, exaltation of larks.

(Sneezes.)

--All of which I'm allergic to.

(Wipes nose.)

Uh. Absolutely disgusting. Excuse me. My head is so full of this kind of thing, if I do not sneeze periodically my brain will blow up. A thousand pardons.

Uh, it is nippy, isn't it? I suppose I look overdressed for country life. No, it's true, nobody comes to a rustic bed & breakfast to wear a white suit. But overdressing does seem to put cold in it's place, doesn't it? "What kind of a

MAN:

lunatic would wear a white suit to the county?! Maybe it's Manhattan, they wear suits anytime there." The art of intimidation. It's the tie. You can't control nature, you can only hope to confuse it with the wrong clothes. Actually, that something that Ted-

(Checks himself. HE looks out doorway.)

They do still serve breakfast here, yes? Yes, alright.

(Sitting at table)

I'd better just claim my territory here, hadn't I? Look like someone who *expects* to be served breakfast anytime, two minutes ago.

(Claps hands. Stares off out through doorway, very focused. Regroups, tries a more intense look. No breakfast is forthcoming.)

Maybe something more expectant.

(Sits up, hands folded, leaning towards door expectantly. Nada.)

Perhaps a come hither approach.

(Strikes a feminine cheesecake pose.)

Mm, something to go with the suit, I think. We are in the land of horseshoes.

(Butch now, "manly" voice.)

Oh yes, we are in the land of horseshoes, barbecues, 4-wheel-drive, manly animal killing and please, mam, leave it rare, I prefer to chew it while it's still squirming! Yeah, run along little lady and bring me some beans -- not pork & beans, not navy, bring me something in *denim*! With a big slab of bloody mammal! And a piping hot cup of antifreeze so if my jeep stalls all I have to do is exhale.

(Drops it, goes to door.)

Well... I can see them but... The service here is not what it was.

(He takes out tiny COMB, does eyebrows and moustache)

MAN:

The people are not what they were. Or, perhaps, it is we I should say, it is I who has changed. Because if this had happened when we we-- when I used to come here, we never w--

(HE pulls back, restates carefully.)

The service here used to be better.

(Looks out door, waits.)

You'd think they would remember… !

(HE removes himself from the frustration, strolls the room with affected casualness, examining decor.)

Well… nevermind. Nothing has really changed in this old place, the old haunt. Except the people & the times. Certainly not the decor.

(Smiles at a long VASE. Slender at the neck, large in body, it hovers somewhere between country kitsch and ornately God awful. HE giggles.)

If you knew what we had –

(Stops himself, puts it back.)

The faces. The faces here have changed.

(Pointing out door.)

Not their faces. They're the same quaint little potato-faces that were always happy to put us up, or put up with us, whatever, as long as we paid, and we did, happily, with all our hearts, here, take it, we had a hell of a time. And one thing about us--

(Redirecting, to stay off the subject.)

One thing about those scary potato-faces: wherever you go outside the city, there's always, like, the same potato-face family, or couple, and that's because, they *are* the same people. Literally, there's seven of them, and they go around and run all the quaint, uncomfortable, out-of-the-way little country things on the whole Eastern seaboard. Oh, they vary their accents,

MAN:

or go from one slightly weird shirt to another, but you're always, inside, when they go by, saying to yourself, "What is wrong with that person? Is it me? Did I wake up with my head inside out? Have my ears sucked onto the inside of my brain or is there just something *off* about him?" Nobody ever really had an accent like that. Or the women's breasts are just.. nobody ever really had breasts like that. And you get out here, and it gets dark, and they disappear. And you're huddling inside wondering, "What do they do out here? At night? By themselves?" I mean, they're not procreating, they can't be, there's only *seven* of them! And *what* is the matter with them? Surely if any of them were sane, they would sell *off* the farm, move to Soho, get some espresso and *good* pastry and have a life! *Please!*

I'm sorry. I could use espresso now, ooh.

> *(Finds pitcher of WATER, pours some)*

Water. Stave off starvation. "He starved, he did *not* dehydrate."

Do I sound provincial, with the espresso thing? Well, my God, that's the worst thing about these people! Ham used to say, to...

> *(Stops, realizes he's brought it up again, de-*
> *cides to go on anyway..)*

To come all the way out here, clear to Mars he used to call it, and find out *they're* just as provincial as you are, oh, that's so irritating! I mean, wake up! If this were the center of the world, New York would be *here*! Helplessly, hopelessly provincial. Teddy--

> *(Veers to the doorway.)*

What is it with these people? Please, if you feed me, I'll leave!

> *(To us)*

Excuse me if I grow antsy --

> *(To outside, trying to catch someone)*

Excuse me!

> *(His call comes too late.)*

Tie and all. No respect for a tie. I wish I was a dyke. They're so tough, they always get served.

MAN:

(HE tries sitting, restless.)

Te -- Somebody I once knew used to sa--

(Tries for less specific)

I once heard the theory...

(This he finds acceptable)

I once heard the theory that the reason it took so long for these potato-faces, which is what we called them, for them to make breakfast is because when you ordered, if you wanted, like potato & eggs, which everybody did, these potato faces had to go into the kitchen, *(does character)* "How many eggs did you want?"

(Mimes breaking eggs)

"There you go! And how much potato?"

(Takes up imaginary peeler and peels own face, laughing.)

"There you go!" I'm sorry. That... That is really so grotesque, but...

(Shakes head)

Sorry. You had to be there.

(HE jumps up and walks OUT doorway.

A long pause. Long.

Finally he comes back, carrying a triumphant BREAKFAST TRAY: Eggs & potatoes, toast rack with English muffin, pot of coffee, butter and jam on a saucer.)

Triumph!

(Makes room on table)

I am a drip! Long live the drips. It is not the raging storm that wears the mountain down, but the gradual, determined, persistent drip, drip, drip! Drip: I am back! Drip: I am dressed! Drip: I have eggs & you-know-whats. Drip: I

MAN:

have muffies in the toast rack, I love a toast rack, very English, tut-tut. And Drip: I... have a coffee pot with no cup. I truly am a drip. Shit.

(Looks around for a cup, waves it off.)

Fuckit. "Where there is a will... there is a Queen in stiletto heels!" Sorry, another inside joke.

(Unloading TRAY.)

I am trying not to do that. There is something profoundly not right about being the only one left inside an inside joke. One must not remain. One must step out. Get up, brush yourself off, and step out of the joke, before you find you are becoming the joke. The tie is optional.

(Sits cheerfully, notes audience.)

I'm sorry, now I'm the only one with food. I hope you'll forgive me, I'm very hungry, I'm going to eat.

(Regards all food with hesitation.)

It's just...everything has a previous... connotation. One can never, ever eat potatoes again, after you've seen somebody do this...

(Peeling gesture again.)

It's so disgusting, he's so g-- he was so gross, he single-handedly...

(Growing rattled.)

It has completely ruined potatoes for me, I don't even eat potatoes in the city. I, I, I don't even...

(Picks up PLATE.)

-- I mean, *look* at that, considering what you know now! Oh, sister, please! Chorusgirl demerit!

(Puts PLATE down as Chorusgirl, executes well-practiced curtsey.)

Thank you so very much. Toast!

MAN:

(Clapping as if calling small children together.)

Children, we will have toast: butter, jam, and beefcake, not necessarily in that order!

(Butters MUFFIN generously)

God, I love butter. Clogs your arteries, slows your brain, gradually disables you and all your kine, hit me with a board, I love butter.

*(Bites muff and chews. Enjoys thoroughly.
Toasts someone invisible. Looks at coffee pot,
then around the room.)*

Okay, class, now comes the arts & crafts portion of our show.

*(Carries COFFEE POT around room looking for
alternative cup. Comes to VASE.)*

If you knew what had been said about this, you wouldn't be able to use it either. Trust me. Vases, potatoes, they sound like a classy bunch, don't they? Oh, honey, you don't know. You don't know what I've lived with. The first time we called ourselves "The Chorusgirls" was the first time we came h-

*(Catches himself, stops, caught dead in the matter
and difficult to change.)*

This is very difficult.

*(HE sits down, pours uses SAUCER for a cop,
pouring coffee.)*

Don't live in the past they tell you, but if that's where you were most alive then it's kind of dead in the present, isn't it? Fuckit, you just float around in the barren, a little disconnected spindly figure. Besides, *I* don't live in the past! *I* am up to date, *I* am pedaling, they just keep overtaking me. I don't think it's my fault, I think it's theirs! I have very inconsiderate dead friends, shame on you all! You all get a demerit and a spanking! -- If you're good..

(HE endeavors to sip coffee from the SAUCER.)

Hm, needs cream. Hm. Rather delicate.

(Goes to door, looks out.)

MAN:

Hello! No, I don't think so. I am not the only one who sees too much of the past hanging off me. Apparently.

(HE returns to coffee. Pours in cream, stirs.)

Surely you've been in this position, even in a minor way, it's bound to get better, don't you think? When you get in a place like this, one of the old haunts, no pun intended, and mostly it belongs to the past, but whether you like it or not you're in the present. And after so long, you have a right to claim it, so what are you going to do? Are you going to go to only new places? Barren, cold uncut territory where there are no handholds to help you through? Are you never to have the comfort and warmth of the old familiar? Do you think it's a kind of giving in? To want to own again some of the places you broke in all together, just so you can rest your feet in old shoes?

I am willing to pay the price of battle with old ghosts. It is to be willing to risk the seduction of memory. Nostalgia is a little like masturbation, you definitely get off on it, the release is real, but the intimacy is all in the mind. You can wake up with a chill.

(Looks at coffee.)

That was so profound I totally forgot what I was talking about. How lucky for you.

(Sips coffee, responds in woman's commercial voice)

"Mm, that's good. Stone cold dead coffee. Try some today."

What was it I just said about masturbation? Not that it really matters, it's just great to have something on hand for those Upper West Side dinners where everyone is just *too* glad to see you and *too* concerned for your story and *too* anxious to ask and they *tilt* their heads just so and it's *so* helpful, and those are the moments you so desperately need something to drop in like, "Masturbation is like..." -- fill in the blank, it doesn't matter what you follow up with, as long as you've said the M-word, each person there has just genetically split down the middle, because their ears have dilated to the size of Nebraska in order to hear every word you have to say about the M, while at the exact same time their minds are going,

(Shaking and covering face)

"Ew, ew, don't talk about it, erase your face, erase your face, hairy palms, spray with Lysol, good clean happy people!"

MAN:

I honestly have always found that enormously funny. You can say "Buttfuck; I'm wearing your underwear from the dirty hamper; and I have your puppy in here with me" and nothing, nothing makes them crawl like just the word. Masturbation. Slapping the salami. Taking the worm for a walk.

> *(Holds up fingers in a circle, moving them up &*
> *down over his lap.)*

"Now put on your leash, No I won't, yes you will, I won't, you will, I won't, you will...! But the worst of all are the people who think it's because you don't live with someone.

> *(In character, hand over mouth)*

"He said the M-word!" "Sh! He's alone now. He has to." "He doesn't have to talk about it!" "Sh!" "Uh, it's disgusting, ew, ach, hairy palms, erase your face, spray with Lysol, good happy clean people!"

> *(Covers eyes. Holds them there.)*

He "does" it.

> *(Brings hands down.)*

Most people do it. Riding a vibrating bus, climbing the rope in gym, or just... looking at a picture until it gives you that oudgy feeling and you trace that feeling with your fingers to see where it comes from, it's not heresy people! Really, in a new age we cannot afford to turn up our noses at any of the options. Teddy s-- people said it's that kind of hypocrisy that allows people to continue dying. "Really, I'm much too sophisticated to masturbate, let's fuck the plague instead."

> *(He stops, hands on knees, reigns himself in,*
> *hurting. He takes a breath, pours more coffee*
> *into his saucer.)*

Elysian Fields. That phrase keeps on coming to mind lately. Elysian Fields. Do you know what that is? Greek paradise. At somebody's memorial -- I'm not sure who's, and that's not crass it's just quantity, and they're so alike, I'm sorry but it's true, but it was Ham or John Paulie or Abe Feinman, one of the literary vigilantes slash Nam vets, and someone read the deceased's state-ment -- this happens more often these days -- I can tell you in the beginning, when people first started to die, there were no noble postmortem epistles read at their funerals because they all they would have read like, "What the fuck is going on?!?" "Dearly Bereaved: I died of a common cold!! Does this

MAN:

happen?!?" "My last will and testament: To my b------ (croaks on table) --
Wait! I'm not done!

(Bangs on table as if trying to get back in to life)

"Really! Hello! I want a refund! I want a refund and a whole new body! One
with a washboard stomach. Okay, I want a refund, a new washboard-
stomach body, and I want a different death this time. Like, 'pushed in front of
a subway' or 'firing squad' or 'torn apart by lions', something easy this time!
Or, no, I have it, 'poisoned by stinking stone-dead cold coffee--"

(Holding saucer out to audience.)

Does someone want this? Really, I can't. Here, this should be for Ham, for
the whole potato debacle, yes!...

(Stands holding up coffee saucer, presenting to the ether.)

Ham, wherever you are, old dear, this is for you.

*(He slurps coffee off saucer, opens coffee pot,
faux barfs it back in, holds up pot)*

Coffee, Gents? Come and get it!

(Pouring it back into saucer)

Ham, please, you're the guest of honor, after you.

(Stops, leans on table, smart.)

There. I hope that stays with you through all eternity. As the potatoes will
stay with me. That's how my postmortem will read: "Dear Friends, as you
view my body today, just know, I never got over the potatoes. Think of me
and weep whenever you see a Mr. Potato Head."

*(He leans over and makes face peeling gesture
over the plate, laughing. He grabs an old
photograph off the wall of a line of stiff standing, ill-fitting old men.)*

And here! This is all of us as bogus old men! Teddy laughed so hard at this
he almost threw up -- really, literally, very weak digestion...

(He hunts through picture, pointing)

MAN:

This is Ham, because he said he's the one with the superior genes, he'd still have the good posture and the full head. Of hair, I'm just quoting him.

(Points at figure in picture)

Here's James & Andy, obviously together, note the perpetual physical contact, even at 90 and 104.

(Points)

Blanco. Apparently he didn't grow the mustache till much later in life because at 38 he couldn't grow peach fuzz, and isn't he a snappy dresser, hm? Love the shorts, Blanco!

(Points)

David Binary, who could forget that smile? Who could know you'd have no teeth at 70?

(Points)

Yes, here's me!

(Laughs at picture)

Ham said he had my frown, because... because when I'm really, really mad, it looks like my eyebrows are... are trying to eat my face!

(Recovers laughing, points)

Excuse me. Let's see, uh, Oh! This was either John Paulie, because of the knees, serious running, or John Steidel because of the shoulders -- Oh God, the shoulders!

(Pointing)

And there's Teddy. Because of the eyes, Ham said. The gentle baby blues. *Nobody* had sweeter eyes, everybody, even Ham, nobody could argue that. And what a miracle of modern science, folks, a full head of hair as an old man, yet bald when he died at 41.

> *(He stops, freezes. Glued to the picture as to a hot coal. He causes himself to be casual, stop looking, tap the frame, put the photo back up on the wall. He stands for a moment rubbing his hands slowly, looking emptily in the direction of his shoes, looking toward the window. He draws to the window, mutters out.)*

MAN:

Raging chaos. No placement.

(He leans looking out.)

Elysian Fields. There's that phrase again. Elysian. Oh, I was telling you about whosy's memorial, the afterword, "Now so-and-so will read a few words from the deceased." -- and I know it was Blanco Goshin who read it, even though he looked like hell, but he was still alive after John and Abe Feinman wasn't -- well, fuckit, who the hell knows? Does anybody here know when Abe Feinman died, just raise your hand -- I know it was after AZT because he had the whole black-market thing and then--fuckit. Whoever the hell died, they said something really memorable and if this takes much longer no doubt somebody else will be dead and having a memorial and I'll have to go and I won't know what the fuck I was talking about. So, in the interest of my sanity, it was Blanco reading, and somebody else's funeral, I don't know who but they were good because they had written, "I feel like, in my life, I found the Elysian Fields. And they turned out to be minefields."

I's really weird when you're talking about what so-and-so said at their funeral when you're busy planning your own. Teddy actually asked me if that was him or was he quoting from somebody else's death? Well, uh, sweetie, let's see now, we know you're not quoting Ham because he had dementia in the end and didn't write a statement. It's a mercy, dementia. He doesn't know you to say goodbye and he's sitting in a pile of his own excrement, but he thinks he's in a hotel on tour, so he's happy. I brought him opening night roses three times. "Break a leg in Chicago, Ham!" "Break a leg in Philly, Ham!" "Break a leg in Boston, Ham!" Wouldn't he have written a great statement for his memorial though? "Dear Family & Friends: by the time you read this, I will be playing Chicago! Please tell all your friends." I wish I could have convinced him it was pre-Broadway.

(He comes out of his trance, steps away from window.)

Well. Well, well, well! This is a bore! I am becoming a big, fat boor!

(Pinches his waist).

Pinch an inch? Yes. I need to eat Special K.

(He reaches in pocket, going into commercial)

"Fat and boring? Nothing becomes you more than stinky carcinogens!"

(Takes out a cigarette.)

MAN:

Hey, if you can't hear five queers yelling "coffin nail" at me right now, I'm crazy. Look, I'm standing in a corner, I have an ashtray, and I'm opening a window.

> *(He opens window, lights cig, takes long satisfy-ing drag.)*

At no time can you *feel* your lungs more than when you smoke. That's a fact. Teddy's reply to that —

> *(Stops himself, frustrated.)*

God, I am a bore. I'm really trying to not do that. I'm really trying. It's very difficult.

> *(Smokes a moment in pregnant silence. Then rushes it out.)*

I'm really trying not to but I'll just tell you because he was a very interesting and witty person when I said at no time can you feel your lungs more than when you smoke he said at no time can you feel your knee caps more than when you stand with them both in the direct path of a live rotary blade, I'll say no more!

> *(He hasn't actually gotten an ashtray, and now needs one. He studies the possibilities, choos-es the spittoon, puts it on the table, taps ash.)*

It's alright, you can use it for this. That's why you can't use it for coffee. God help the potato-face that decides to see what's inside here. Eight and a half years' worth of chicken gristle, chewed gum, cigarette ash and roach butts. Ham used to come down and smell it in the morning to gage how much of a good time we'd had the night before. This was helpful when you couldn't quite remember yourself. Thermometer of Thrills.

> *(Smells it)*

"Ah. 8.5: moderate blow out."

> *(Smells it)*

Ew. Straight 9: serious fun, late night."

> *(Smells it)*

"Aach! That's putrid! We had *so* much fun! 10's across the board!"

*(He laughs, daintily clears the table onto the tray,
referring to spittoon)*

MAN:

So, that is another one of those things. It has significance. Everything has a connotation. Meaning. The longer you live, or the more people that die, it seems the more things and place take on connotations, so little is just what it is, everything has a memory tied up in it already because somebody did something once, made it a Thrill Thermometer or whatever, so that even something just even similar is still going to remind you, and now *it* has meaning, and the first person you ever know that dies, you want to keep his things forever, all of them, the pictures and the records and the knickknacks because it reminds you of him, and because he meant something to you and if he's really gone forever, by God, you can stave off mortality for him in this way, just a little bit of him, show a little bit of loyalty by holding his knickknacks above the tide: I *wear* his shirts, I *knew* him! And the same with somebody else you knew that died, and for the second and third people you happen to know who die, whether you knew him or her well, they were members of the flock, you owe 'em, so you use the lamp. It signifies.

And if you lose a number of people over the years you begin to take less and reject more, you resent it, like these things, these mementos, take on a weight of their own, like they're sodden with memory, and all of your most comfortable places are beginning to be full of faces that aren't there but still take up room, making so much of your life too laden to use! So you go to the new places and do the new things, but they're sterile strangers, nobody has used them or broken them in for you or warmed them up with a laugh, so much now is like new shoes that don't feel like you. You can't remember anymore... where the glass came from...

Surely you must have some sense of what I'm talking about, even once, of wanting something of someone's because you loved them, this was that person, you knew them now they're gone but it's... got... fingerprints... There's a presence of death. The.. fingerprints of dread, on the glass itself like plague and it can give it to you and you never want to touch anything again, but if you don't, you'll die.

I cleaned out a dead man's apartment once in an hour and a half. Clothes plates food shoes photos shirts sheets paperwork medication keys. His life. Less time than a movie. I could probably do it for your place. You certainly never know. They looked at me like I was coldhearted.

I don't know if you have ever had a significant person in your life die. A sister or a brother or a parent or a heart's dearest. It wasn't any different for me. I know some people still think it is. I really think the homosexual thing makes it more like... a cat. Or a sheep. No sense rushing into legislation for mere

MAN:

sheep. Teddy said at the time, "They're calling it *our* disease! They don't want to give us any legislation, but they're more than happy to give us our own disease!" Thank you so much.

But I assure you. In the last few hours that I held Teddy in my arms, just as you would, the only difference was I wondered if I had had enough left inside me to let him know how much his absence would mean.

> *(He sits silently. After a time, wipes his eyes and*
> *sighs, finally more peaceful. He takes out a*
> *cigarette, lights it.)*

He got me to stop smoking. Whose lover doesn't. But this is okay, I told him after he died I'd probably start again because, hey, after your house is burnt down, who gives a shit if the floor is clean.

> *(Picks up tray.)*

I wish they would come and take this.

> *(He puts it near the door, stares off.)*

Really I'd like a real cup of coffee. I love coffee. Buttered muffin, coffee. I'm a happy man. Coffee person. I hate tea people. They all are working with limited potential. If you are a tea person, let me say this to you. Life can get better.

Teddy said that it was okay to start again because after I was done grieving and had some time I could stop again. And that was very comforting because it made me feel he could see it. That he'd mowed the lawn for me a little way ahead. At least he goes up to there. He's with me up to that point. And that's good.

Who knows, maybe I will die by that time. Although, I don't know, I don't seem to die. But maybe by then I will have, and if I'm dead then I have to tell you something. You.. will have... to live... with this!

> *(He puts the spittoon the table.)*

And this...

> *(Puts the photo on the table.)*

And this, God help you!

> *(Puts the plate of eggs & potatoes on the table)*

MAN:

My friends, even this.

> *(Puts the saucer on the table. Looks at*
> *audience.)*

Try. Just try to forget. If you had only a rotten time, you had maybe a chance. But, I'm sorry, somewhere, at least in the beginning of my ramblings, you had a little fun, it got you just a little. Well, now they're marked. All of them. You won't even be able to see anything similar.

> *(Signifying spittoon.)*

You'll see a vase and it will be tall and you'll, you won't be able to stop yourself. You're marked. I've marked you. Somewhere, inside, even just a little. Even with them.

> *(Adds picture of old men to the collection.)*

I've cursed you with them. The old men we will never be. We laughed so hard, and you know it now, that Blanco almost wet his pants and Teddy literally almost threw up. Very lovely. Well... it makes a difference.

> *(He looks out to audience genuinely.)*

If it doesn't now, it will.

Well, I must go upstairs and have myself a little rest. I do hope I haven't bored you to tears, but then again, if I have, what the fuck are you gonna do? Oh, look! I love it!

> *(He grabs a delicate, friendly little "No Smoking*
> *Please" sign, previously totally unseen. He adds*
> *that to the table.)*

An obnoxious boor is the freest person on earth. Heigh-ho, world!

> *(Makes a farting gesture and sound. He sighs,*
> *walks toward the door.)*

It's been a pleasure, I hope I see you again.

> *(He stops, looks at spittoon.)*

And who can say?

(He strolls back, takes a last drag off the cigarette, and with a mischievous smile, drops the butt into the spittoon.)

MAN:

It's only half an hour till lunch.

(HE turns and walks out.)

CASTING TABLE, WOMEN'S ROLES

~ D R A M A ~		
Monologue	*Character/Circumstance*	*Page*
Such Stuff as Dreams Are Made on	Director addresses cast at first read-through	1
But When We Saw Each Other	Former prostitute falls in love	4
Just Another Lump in the Ice	Rampage on the futility of violence	13
Saved By a Moonbeam	Captive describes source of survival	18
Sex in a Bar Bathroom	Recovered alcoholic on alienation	27
No Purpose At All	Victorian spinster laments future	30
The Nameless Lips	Sexually compulsive on her source of despair	34
It's All Absurd	Single Victorian about finding a man	36
I Remember What it is to Be Close	Loner recalls good sex	40
The Bone Counter	Seduction through creepy story	41
Something Divine	Apology from window ledge	44
This is How We Did it	Senior lesbian on social revolution	45
I Stood For love	Broken hearted makes stand	47
Shitty, Painful & Bitter	Teen runaway describes attack	49
Before Gals	Drunk and burned by a guy	
She's Got the Name	Prisoner disassociates from self	52
78 Horses	Shut-in describes what is of value	54
Helping Me With a Painting	Neurotic painter asking for help	55
Too Many to Count	Obsessive Compulsive Disorder	58
A Short Thread	Dealing with sister's euthanasia	59
Life Becomes Art	An artist describes the challenge	61
~ C O M E D Y ~		
Guava	Conflicted attraction	2
I Feel My Fingers Creeping About My Face	Compulsive need to make faces at her husband	5
Sex in Droves	Lonely & drunk, resenting other's joy	8
Love is Like a Rare Bird	Meek woman wants to save love	19
The Deeds Good Do-Bees Do	Country gal on doing what you were meant to	20
Take a Pill or Something	Anti-Feminist begs off causes	22
Dropped & Bopped	Failing to scatter lover's ashes	23
The Course a Love	Crank forced to make a toast to love	31
HellDevil	Young lesbian loses temper at old cranky dyke	32
Lesbian-ish	Married woman conflicted on orientation	50

CASTING TABLE, MEN'S ROLES

~ D R A M A ~

Monologue	Character/Circumstance	Page
Such Stuff as Dreams Are Made on	Director addresses cast at first read-through	1
The Hole	Social worker losing sense of purpose	3
You Gotta Have Somethin'	Comfort in a lonely life	9
I Hate Your Heart	Bitter longing at getting left	10
Deberiamos Estar Abajo en el Cementerio!	Rage vs. celebration of life (Spanish version)	14
We Should Be Down in the Graveyard!	Rage vs. celebration of life (English version)	16
I Got to Lay You Down	Releasing the ghost of his brother	21
You Will Feel the Breeze	Guardian Angel recruits scammer	24
A Wonderful Emptiness	On falling in love	25
Someplace In Mexico	Completely lost, literally & figuratively	26
Batman	Condemned man, not bright	33
Two Little Ganoods	Angry, betrayed & sexist	37
I Want You to Pilot	Teaching a man to fly imaginative space ship	38
Masks	Sly Frenchman on the uses of disguise	39
Thermometer of Thrills	Gay man on the significance of loss	42
Every Wavelength Has its Limits	Shallow talk show host confronted with meaning	46
I Let Go	Soldier who loves the earth discovers he's dead	48
Down Deep Where the Serpents Roll	Losing it as he describes how he deals with mentally ill sister	53
Elysian Fields	On attending memorials	56
When I Go	Last speech before execution	61

~ C O M E D Y ~

Do You Know What Happened to Me Today?	Catty anti-social recounts running into a friend from third grade	7
Bob Bean on Justice	Baffled philosopher espouses on justice	11
Keg-o-rama	Plans go awry for college dunce	51
Makin' Worlds	Pothead tech director loves theater	57

To Tom Johnson, for his readings, editing, acting, and friendship.

To Alfonso Ramirez for his help & generosity. And to Eileen Weiss, for her spontaneous gesture of faith with the ISBN number.

And to Melba, who always believes.

And to the Artists and Companies who presented the original productions of many of the included works. Thank you...

DUCKS CROSSING
Produced by Vital Theatre Company, Steven Sunderlin Artistic Director - Directed by Julie Hamberg • Featuring Anna Ewing Bull, Tasha Guevara, Katherine Gooch, Tom Johnson, G.R. Johnson, Jon Krupp, Carolyn Popp, George Sheffey, Casey Stewart-Lindley, Mark Watson - Lighting Design by Aaron Spivey, Set by Heather Dunbar.

FRIENDS OF THE DECEASED
Originally produced by Circle East Theatre Company, Michael Warren Powell Artistic Director, at HERE - Directed by David Title • Featuring Tanya Berezin & Tammy Trull. Subsequently produced at the Vital Theatre Company - Directed by Andrea 'Spook' Testani • Featuring Pamela Dunlap & Vanessa Shealy.

EATING THE DEAD
Produced by Live Theater at Centerstage, Melanie Armer Artistic Director - Directed by Melanie Armer • Featuring Jeremy Briesel, Danielle Delgado, Johnny Sanchez, Michele Torres, and Katherine Wallach. - Set Design by Chris Jones • Lighting Design Tyler Micoleau.

FIONA'S MANE
Originally produced at The Women's Project , Julia Miles Artistic Director - Directed by Michele Coleman • Featuring Jo Twiss. Subsequently produced by The LAB Theatre Company at the Westbank Theatre - Directed by Michele Coleman • Featuring Russell Jones & Nancy Snyder.

GLASS JAW
Produced by The Barrow Group at their Studio Theater, Seth Barrish & Lee Brock Artistic Directors - Directed by Donna Jean Fogel • Featuring Tom Johnson, George Sheffey & Jane Shepard - Light & Set design by Travis McHale, Sound designed & created by Mat Busler.

GOD IS A DYKE
Produced by The LAB Theatre Company at the Westbank Theatre - Directed by Julie Hamberg • Featuring Donna Jean Fogel.

THE GOOD DRUM
Produced by Circle East Theater Company at the HERE Space - Directed by Jane Shepard • Featuring Sir George Sheffey.

HELLEDEN
Produced at Wings Theatre - Directed by Jane Shepard • Featuring Michael Matts, Kenneth Simmons, Julie Shepard, Dennis Stanton, Sean Butler, Kenneth Starr (aka Joel Parsons (remembered with love), and Mark McClain Wilson

THE IDIOT'S GUIDE TO THE BRAIN
Written with the generous support of Sloan Foundation Grant and originally presented by Ensemble Studio Theatre through their First Light Series, with gratitude to J. Holtham.

Subsequently produced at Vital Theater Company as part of *"This Is Your Brain On..."* Produced by Julie Hamberg - Directed by Frank Pisco, who is remembered with love • Featuring Jane Shepard.

THE LAST NICKEL
Previously titled "Anybody's Game", produced at One Dream Theatre, Laine Valentino Artistic Director - Directed by Julie Hamberg • Featuring Kate Bennis, Jack Nagel, George Sheffey & Jane Shepard.

LONG DISTANCE
Originally produced by Vital Theatre Company, Steve Sunderlin Artistic Director - Directed by Frank Pisco • Featuring Stewart Clarke. Subsequently produced by Circle East Theatre Company, Michael Warren Powell Artistic Director, at HERE – Directed by Frank Pisco • Featuring Stewart Clarke.

NINE
Originally produced at the Cornelia Street Café - Directed by Gregor Paslawsky • Featuring Joan Rater & Jane Shepard. Produced at Wings Theatre • Directed by Jane Shepard • Featuring Molly Powell & Jessica Weglein. Subsequently produced at the Circle Rep Lab - Directed by Michele Coleman • Featuring Kit Flanagan & Donna Jean Fogel.

ONE MOLECULE
Produced by The LAB Theatre Company at Circle in the Square Theatre - Directed by Melanie Armer • Featuring Kate Bennis & Linda Larson. Produced again by Circle East Theater Company at Chashama Theatre - Directed by Ken Lowstetter • Featuring Meg Anderson & David Folwell.

A RAGE OF CHAOS
Originally produced at the Cornelia Street Café & moved to Wings Theatre - Directed by Jane Shepard • Featuring Gregor Paslawsky. Subsequently produced by The LAB Theatre Company at the Westbank Theatre - Directed by Melanie Armer • Featuring Michael Warren Powell. This production was also seen at Judson Church, The Duplex, and the Carmel Festival for the Performing Arts.

PRELUDE TO WALKING
Produced by The LAB Theatre Company at Circle in the Square Theatre - Directed by Michele Coleman • Featuring Suzan Postel & Lou Sumrall. – Moved for a run at Synchronicity Space,.

REAP THE WILD HISTORIAN
Produced by Circle East Theatre Company at Chashama - Directed by David Title • Featuring Nell Mooney and Jane Shepard.

SUBWAY
Produced by the Next Theatre Company at The Producer's Club - Directed by Andrea 'Spook' Testani • Featuring Colleen Davenport & Kit Flanagan.

If you enjoyed this work, check out these other rockin' independent playwrights & plays

"Floating" by Shawn Hirabayashi
Find it at: Hirabayashi@hotmail.com

"Pumpkins For Smallpox" by Catherine Gillet
Find it at:. www.nytesmallpress.com/pp03.php
In "Plays and Playwrights 2003" by Martin Denton

"Anything For You" by Catherine Clesia Allen
Find it at: www.amazon.com/Take-Ten-New-10-Minute-Plays/dp/0679772820
in "Take Ten, New Ten-Minute Plays"

"I Dream Before I Take the Stand" by Arlene Hutton
Find it at: www.playscripts.com

"How To Roast a Pepper" by Ty Adams
via www.lightcatcher.org

"Night Visits" by Simon Fill
Find it at: www.actorstheatre.org/humana_anthologies.htm
in "Ten Minute Plays From Actor's Theater of Louisville, Volume 6"

"Parading With Nell" by Annie Evans
Find it at *http://www.lulu.com/content/278057*
in "Funny Girls Coping With Boys"

"178 Head" by C. Denby Swanson
Find it at: maura.teitelbaum@abramsartny.com
in "2004: The Best Ten Minute Plays for 3 or more Actors"

Also by Jane Shepard...

Available at

www.Kickass-plays.com

Blessings.

Made in the USA
San Bernardino, CA
14 August 2018